More Advance Praise for Slade Ham's

UNTIL ALL THE DRAGONS ARE DEAD

"It's all too easy to walk dead-eyed through this weird little narrow life & sometimes we need some half-mad prophet to shake us out of the sand. Who better than a globetrotting, midget-wrestling, uptight-realtor-pranking, hot-shot comedian? Slade's a funny guy, no doubt, but past the laughter are the beautiful hard lessons of living wide open, full-out, until every last dragon lies dead. God bless Texas & God bless Slade Ham."

—Jamie Blaine, author of *Midnight Jesus*

"Slade could have been a lot of things, but the world is glad he found comedy and writing. He's gifted at it. Besides, he'd have been a lousy starship captain. They have to know math."

—Alonzo Bodden, comedian

"They say that to understand a man's journey, you must walk a mile in his shoes. After reading Slade Ham's new memoir of curious vignettes, I feel as though I have acid-tripped through a multidimensional time warp of bizarre tales, spanning the far reaches and nether regions of the known universe, laughing my ass off and straining my cheeks through every page. Not only do I think I understand him, I think I want to be him."

—Burton C. Bell, lead singer of Fear Factory

"Slade writes his adventures like Mark Twain, if Twain had been a road act willing to go to jail just for the joke. He leaves no doubt about why he's one of the best standups working today, or why he is probably the real 'Most Interesting Man in the World.'"

—Tammy Pescatelli, comedian

"Grab a bottle of Jameson and your 20-sided die and settle in for a subversive ride only Slade Ham could deliver. With prose that leaps off the page and heartfelt stories that you have to read to believe, *Until All the Dragons Are Dead* will thrill and delight, and make you realize life is too short to spend it growing up."

—Richard Cox
Author of *The Boys of Summer* and *Thomas World*

"Slade Ham is first-class company: a globetrotting guy's guy incapable of dullness, with a good heart and a code of honor besides. I know this because I've been lucky enough to hang out with him, and now you can do the same with *Until All the Dragons Are Dead*, though you will have to supply your own whiskey. But that's the only thing missing. Yes, please keep slaying those dragons, Slade. I'll help. And you're going to want to pitch in, too."

—Duke Haney
Author of *Subversia* and *Banned for Life*

"Slade is the funniest 'not funny' man I know! I love you, bud."

—Kevin Martin, lead singer of Candlebox

"Not many supposedly funny people are actually that funny, but this kid cracks me up. All day long. If I ever need a funny joke, I'll call Slade. If I ever need a funny story from the night before told right, I'll call Slade. Speaking of which, did you tell 'em the one about the gym lights yet?"

—Scarface, The Geto Boys

"I was lucky to travel the Middle East with Slade and I never witnessed him without a smile. He sees each day as a new adventure, and these stories embody his *joie de vivre*. That is French for something. I don't speak French. But Slade must have a hole in his bucket list, because he is continuously living out his dreams, and the stories of his adventures are as inspirational as they are funny."

—Jordan Brady
Director of the *I Am Comic* documentary trilogy

Until All the Dragons Are Dead

To Jo –
Two countries &
counting!

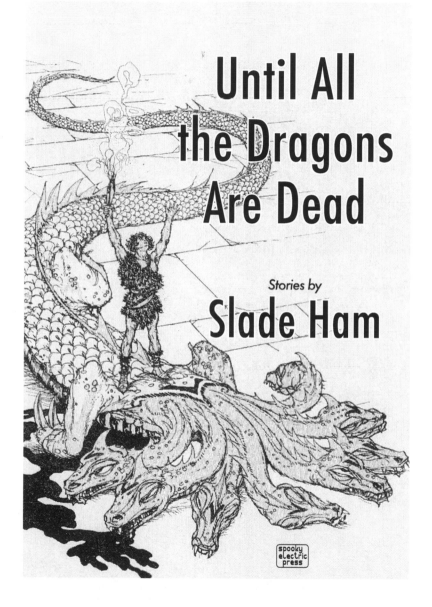

Until All the Dragons Are Dead

Stories by

Slade Ham

spooky
electric
press

Published by Spooky Electric Press

First Edition, 2018

Copyright © 2018 Slade Ham

Cover Image: *Contes roses* by Charles Robert-Dumas. Page 94.
Published 1914 by Boivin, Paris. Courtesy New York Public Library.

Book Design: Charlotte Howard, CKH Design, Boston, MA
The text is set in Caslon. The titling is Futura.

ISBN 978-0-69-209465-5

Printed in the United States of America

To my father, who saw the genesis of things, but none of the success. I miss you, old man.

CONTENTS

FOREWORD

Words have a power that nothing else does, and when you put the right words in the right order, they can change a nation, explain the universe, or, most importantly, make you laugh. Slade Ham, who has been a friend of mine for years, has taken the time and effort to put together the right words, in the right order, to explain his inexplicable life.

I laughed, hard. On top of being funny, his storytelling is impeccable. Slade takes you through his world, and the ENTIRE world in this (I hate to use the word, but,) "romp" through a whiskey-soaked adventurer's life. The stories are Hunter S. Thompson, meets comic book geek, meets post-modern clown. I loved it. From *Possessed Hippos* to *MMA Midgets*, the laughter was non-stop, as was the little bit of pain that only life as a continent-hopping "Comedy Pirate" can bring.

The planet today is a tough place, but Slade has flown through it on steel falcons, vanquishing personal dragons, slinging booze and making drunk people howl with laughter. His stories are harrowing, heartfelt, and hilariously wrong. The power of a man is never in his fists, although Slade uses both of his with an often ridiculous effect. The true power of a man lies in his words, and Slade's words are funny and full of insight, which is something we desperately need now — at least until all the dragons are dead.

—Christopher Titus
January 10, 2018

PROLOGUE:
WHEN I GROW UP

What do you want to be when you grow up? They always ask you that when you're younger. I never knew how to answer it, mainly because answering it implied that I had to accept growing up at all. My parents encouraged me to play outside, the product of having four boys and a desperate need for some privacy. When they divorced and my mom took custody we spent even more time outside.

I was a ninja before I was ten, climbing on neighbors' roofs and scaling fences. My brothers and I made masks from old black shirts and crept silently through the night when we were supposed to be sleeping. I stalked through the November woods, crunchy, cold, and grey, a Knight of the Round Table looking for dragons to fight. A shed at the end of the road was a pirate's hideout, a place to build booby traps. It was musty and damp and the air tasted like wet wood, and it was the perfect place for an eleven-year-old to hide from the real world.

When I was 13, I found *Star Trek: The Next Generation* and began obsessively building starships. I sketched them in my eighth grade notebooks and built them out of Legos in the bedroom I shared with my middle brother. I watched Commander Mark create his *Secret City* on PBS, and it made me pick up a pencil for the first time. Then came comic books. Todd McFarlane's version of Spider-man inspired me to continue drawing. Erik Larsen, Jim Lee, Mark Bagley, Rob Liefeld, Marc Silvestri, Mike Mignola, Sam Keith — they all encouraged me to create worlds of my own. My paper-covered textbooks were emblazoned with the images of superheroes. Ghost Rider burned brightly on the fronts of my folders and Wolverine's claws sliced cleanly through the back. It never occurred to me that the blonde cheerleader I'd had a crush on since the fifth grade wasn't into those sorts of things.

During my sophomore year of high school we were tasked with creating a presentation detailing a society of our own design. It was supposed to have a government and an economic system and a basic infrastructure. Not every child's dream project, but not every child was me. The assignments were turned in a month later, with most of the student's projects existing on a single piece of poster board displaying the most basic elements of civilization. Their citizens were dead. Lifeless. They lived in a colorless, cardboard world. How could anyone allow themselves to create anything with such a lack of passion? It made me angry.

I, along with my friends Trey and Garret, had spent the entire month piecing together a 100-page book about our civilization. Metallica's *Black Album* had just come out, and as *Don't Tread On Me* thumped in the background, we detailed the history of a star gone nova and the surviving eight societies that emerged from it.

There were illustrations and technical guides and ancient documents and trade agreements and uneasy alliances. It was a masterpiece.

I've obviously been a huge nerd for most of my life, you may begin to gather.

I buried myself in books while my classmates went to parties. Twain, Dumas, Stevenson, Carroll and Barrie took me on adventures when I should have been trying to talk to that cheerleader. My small group of friends was enough for me, when they'd have me.

I got in fights at lunch in both middle school and high school because I've never known when to shut my mouth. I was quick to throw a punch, and even better at taking one. I fought one kid, Ben, at least eight times between the sixth and ninth grades. We were Ali and Frazier on a playground. I got rocked by a muscle-cut black teen on the bus one day because he thought I tripped him. The truth was, he was being an asshole and I did trip him, I just didn't know he'd seen me do it. I took a quick right hook to the mouth that day that split my bottom lip against my braces. I don't think the bus driver even slowed down.

High school ended and college began. They asked me again: What do you want to be? My dad had convinced me that I wanted to be a Civil Engineer despite my inability to get past Algebra 2 before the 12th grade. I understood math but I hated it. Here's everything I know about the value of x: combined with 25 other letters, it is capable of telling magnificent stories. No matter how many times my dad tried to explain the importance of the career he'd chosen for me, I couldn't stop asking the same question. "Why should I do something I don't like to do?"

"Because you have to," they said, and I went back to drawing on my book cover.

I dropped out after my first year of college and begged a radio station for a job. After months of what probably bordered on harassment, I was finally hired to run the *Rick Dee's Show* on the affiliate in town. I wasn't really on the radio, of course. I just showed up to an empty station every Sunday morning at six o'clock and made sure the CD didn't skip. Unsupervised, however, I taught myself to pick the lock on the production room door, and in that tiny, wood-paneled room, I made mock aircheck tapes and sent them to the competing station across town. They finally caved and gave me a microphone.

Eventually I landed the coveted seven to midnight shift and got to count down the Top 8 modern rock songs. It was a crash course in cool for a kid who had struggled to down two strawberry wine coolers less than a year earlier. Radio can be unstable though, and I went from disc jockey to bartender, and back to disc jockey, while my friends began to get married around me. Evidence of adulthood surrounded me.

Around the same time, I discovered standup comedy and moved in with my girlfriend. We spent a volatile eight years together while I began to fall in love with the world. Comedy allowed me travel, first to a few different states and then eventually to Germany two weeks after September 11th. Soon I was off to corners of the globe I never imagined I'd see. Now, 18 years later, I'm uncomfortable when I'm not moving. I find myself longing to get back home, but a few days after I do I become bored again. I visit my nieces and laugh at the people my friends try to set me up with. I try to explain that the girl next door is never going to work for me, unless the girl next door wants to quit her nine-to-five job and help me flip the world upside down. I savor the time I spend with my family, and then the music starts playing in my head again, pulling me like 10,000 horses back into the dusty streets. There are stories to collect. I need to be out there, wherever there might be.

Every time I get on an airplane or toss my backpack in the backseat for a road trip, I am a kid again. Mighty wooden sword and dog-eared notebook in hand, I have to wander. Sometimes I wonder what it would have been like to have settled in a nice neighborhood back in my hometown, with a regular job and batch of kids running around the house waking me up at six in the morning. I see the people that chose that path and they seem happy enough. I, on the other hand, can't even begin to imagine how I would feel if I had to look forward to the weekend to get my two days of pseudo-freedom. I'm afraid those hypothetical children would have grown up fatherless. I don't think I actually would have left them, but I might have hung myself.

I don't find any fault in that way of life; to do so would be arrogant, and even more arrogant than usual. But I can't find enough right with it to make me want to go that direction either. I wasn't trained for it. I don't have those muscles. I don't vibrate on the same frequency as the people that Snuggie commercials are made for. I would die in that world almost certainly, like a baby dropped off in the Congo.

But I know how to play. That's what I do know. It's what I knew best even as a kid, as I was scrawling words in the back of my spiral. I want to tell stories. I want to go out and get them, and then come back and give them to other people. It may never make me rich, but it does make me happy.

I still don't really know what I want to be when I grow up. The things that make me the happiest aren't always obtainable. They are things I stumbled upon while I was exploring, little gemstones buried in the mud that I've partially uncovered but can't quite pry completely out of the ground for one reason or another. I'm allowed to visit them on my journeys, whether certain people or my favorite café or the view from a particular mountain, but only for fleeting moments before I have to sail off again.

So I turn the rock up in my earbuds and toast to the things I am allowed to own — those late nights and shots of whiskey and Third World airports and good arguments and rascal friends and tattered journals and broken people, and most of all, damn good stories.

What follows are a few of them.

HAVE HAPPY DAY

I am boarding a plane in Houston to go see the cherry blossoms in bloom and hop from base to base telling jokes through most of South Korea and Japan. My itinerary is complicated, and the first leg in particular leaves very little space for a mistake. In a perfect world, I am supposed to head for Detroit, catch a connecting flight to Tokyo and continue on to Busan, South Korea.

In a perfect world.

In the real world, where I live, I won't be so fortunate, which is often my fate on the road.

As soon as the cabin door closes, the crew informs us that there is a minor computer issue. "It should only take a few minutes to correct though," the pilot's voice crackles out over the intercom, received by 42 rows worth of sighs. "A few minutes" sounds like a lie. A few is three, and nothing on an airplane takes three minutes.

A baby cries somewhere in front of me. Sweet Jesus, already? The mother feeds it a bottle and rocks it to sleep as "a few minutes" slowly become 60. I sit stuck in my window seat and watch as that window begins to fog up from the lack of air circulation. It's been an hour, I think. It can't be much longer. My finger traces a sad, dripping line through the condensation. I write "Help Me" backwards in the sweat.

I'm a borderline claustrophobic person by nature and being stuck on the inside of a row isn't helping. The massive woman in the aisle seat is the size of an adolescent rhinoceros, dashing any hopes I might have of getting out and moving around. At least I'm not in the middle, I comfort myself.

That seat belongs to a man in his 40s, who, while having said nothing to support this characterization, carries himself with a holier-than-thou attitude. I immediately don't like him. He just seems arrogant. Maybe it is the way his facial bones are structured, or maybe it's the reading glasses perched on the tip of his nose like a cliff diver, but he looks like someone who thinks he should have a butler. I bet he would be happier with a monocle. "Simmer down," I want to say. "You're back here in coach with the rest of us."

The clock ticks past an hour and a half.

The speaker rattles again, this time with worse news. "This is your captain again. Umm … we're going to try to get this computer restarted one more time … umm … and if that doesn't work we're going to have to bring a crew on board to replace it. Just sit tight. It shouldn't be much longer," the captain lies again. Captain Liar-Liar-Pants-on-Fire.

Two hours.

Time crawls. I glance at the crumpled boarding pass shoved in my pocket and notice that I only have a three-hour layover scheduled in Detroit before my flight to Japan. This is going to be way too close. I scribble things in my notebook in an attempt to distract myself. The man in the middle begins to get curious. He pushes his glasses up on his better-than-everyone nose and then tries to slyly read what I am writing, as if a radar-less bat couldn't tell what he was doing. I adjust my writing to compensate. I flip over to a fresh page and I start a new paragraph:

"If you don't stop reading this I will stab you in the ear with my pen and hide your body under the large woman to your left. They will never find you, do you understand that? And when I'm through with you, and I get off this godforsaken plane, I will hunt your children down and eat them. You read that right. I will eat your children. On bread. Like a Po' Boy."

He harrumphs and adjusts his gaze.

Three hours.

My layover time is all but gone now. Unless we take off in five minutes, I will miss my next flight. I take a deep breath when I hear the intercom buzz. "Captain Adams here one more time. Just wanted to update you folks on our status. Looks like they have the problem under control. We apologize for keeping you on the plane, but it should only be a couple more minutes. Sit tight."

"Liar!" Someone yells from the back. We all laugh, but it is the laughter of a defeated army.

The beluga whale at the end of our row isn't doing so well. The armrests are not being kind to her hips in an irresistible-force meets immovable-object sort of way. The way she seems stuck in her seat reminds me of a video I once saw where a double-decker bus failed to make it underneath an overpass.

Three and a half hours.

All I can focus on is that I have to get to Detroit. I have to. The Baby Damien is crying again, now awake from its nap. Middle Man is fidgeting uncontrollably next to me but he avoids making eye contact. The sack of mattresses next to him is snoring, though she is wide awake. Her breaths come in erratic gusts, each one sounding more laborious than the last. More crying sounds cut through the thick air. Is that child in a blender? That can't just be one baby. This is miserable. I hope this plane blows up, I think to myself.

Four and a half hours.

We are all beaten. Even the flight attendants have given up any semblance of professionalism. Ties loosened and sweat dripping, they drag a beat up water cart down the center aisle. "Just say something if you want some more water," one of them mutters. "I can't help you otherwise."

Five hours.

My connecting flight took off almost two hours earlier. "Good news," the captain interrupts. "We've resolved the problem and are cleared for takeoff."

179 people sigh in relief. The fat lady just keeps trying to breathe.

I make it through Detroit and into Tokyo eventually, trudging into Narita Airport around 11:30 at night. A clerk informs me that the last flight into Busan has already taken off, but that they will happily fly me to Seoul for the night. "We get you hotel, and drive person will arrive to transport you," the lady behind the counter says in broken English. "Here ticket. Go enjoy. Have happy day."

All of Korea goes to bed well before midnight. I learn this upon arriving at Incheon Airport in Seoul. Apparently they're like Monchhichis in that regard; at ten o'clock, someone takes the jewels out of their bellies and they fall fast asleep. The airport is huge and devoid of people. I am Tom Cruise in *Vanilla Sky* if, too tired to run, he had skipped directly to the screaming-at-the-sky-and-spinning-in-a-circle part. How could the airport be empty? Where is my driver? I still have to get a hold of someone in Busan and let them know that I am not going to make it. The only contact information I have is for a man mysteriously named "Mr. O." I have that, and a phone number with a thousand digits.

I have no Korean *won* and the Currency Exchange has long since closed. I stumble down the massive hallway, delirious, trying to make sense of the logograms that surround me. My exhausted mind translates them based on their appearance: picnic table, telephone pole, tree house. I am getting nowhere quite quickly.

One lone sentry waits by the exit near an eerily silent baggage claim. He leads me to a phone and I convince him to leave a message for Mr. O before he leaves me standing there alone. I have been up for nearly 30 hours. Where is my ride to the hotel? A voice echoes my thought even as it occurred.

"Hotel?" I hear someone say.

I am certain that I am imagining things because there is no one there. "Hotel?" the voice says again, and then a four-foot-tall Korean man appears from behind an abandoned counter.

"Yes," I say. "Please." I don't even care if he is the right guy or not. I just want to stand under a hot shower and maybe take a nap.

"Come. We go fast," he grins.

"Yes," I reply. "Fast is good."

He leads me to a van, throws my bag in the passenger side, and then clambers into the driver's seat. I slide open the side door and crawl into my seat in the back, ready to doze off until we reach our destination. I hear the ignition fire up as my eyes close, and then I snap them back open again as Korean rap explodes from the speakers. It sounds like a machine gun that shoots words at your face. I'd rather hear that baby again than this.

The van tires squeal, kicking up dust, and we shoot forward in the dark outskirts of Seoul at the speed of sound.

He sits on three encyclopedia-sized books and can still barely see over the steering wheel. I pull myself forward against the g-force to see how fast we're going, forgetting that the speedometer is showing kilometers. Through the windshield I can see the dimly illuminated road. Apparently we only have one headlight, like the Wallflowers. Another car appears ahead of us, but only for a moment. My driver bump drafts them as we fly past, and throws his hands in the air like the kid in *The Neverending Story* that rode that big, flying dog. *"Mansae!"* he yells.

I move to the center of the bench seat and put on all three seatbelts.

We slide to a halt in front of the hotel like the end of a rollercoaster, and I crawl out of the van shaking and happy to be alive. He pushes my bag out after me, yells something else in Korean, and rockets off into the night.

"Have happy day," I chuckle.

I'll never know exactly how fast we actually went. I know we covered what I estimated to be 1,100 miles in about 18 minutes, and I can't help but wonder where that guy was when I needed to get from Houston to Detroit 30 hours ago.

UNTIL ALL THE DRAGONS ARE DEAD

I have a tree house. I built it, unapologetically, as an adult, and while it was borne of necessity it has since become something bigger. For the last few years I've been living in an apartment complex owned and managed by an ancient woman who hardly knows who lives in her building, much less what any of us are up to. There aren't a ton of restrictions on what you can or cannot do in this complex, and even if there were there is no one here to enforce them.

Over the years I've become good friends with several of the other residents. I am living with my girlfriend Brittany right now, and I am constantly looking for a reason not to be in the apartment with her. Our relationship is what you might call explosive. The less I am here, the less chance of inadvertently setting off an emotional truck-bomb, so I spend a good bit of time hanging out with our ragtag group of neighbors.

Dan is your typical Southeast Texas redneck. About six-foot-four, he drinks cheap beer by the case, drives a pickup truck, and eats weird things if you dare him. I personally watched him consume a raw shrimp and three wrinkled dollar bills one night simply because someone bet him a dollar. He ate three of his own dollars to win one of someone else's. Dan lives across the street from Chuck, a gun-collecting Texan with a bit more intelligence. Dan is the kind of guy that will beat his chest and tell you what he is going to do. Chuck will just do it.

And Chuck happens to live next door to Henry. Henry is a stout and stocky black guy. Permanently high, he is the kind of person you can't help but like. He is Ice Cube in *Friday*.

Over the course of the summer, a group of teens has chosen our neighborhood as a target for a string of car burglaries. My car has been hit twice along with eleven other incidents in the last few weeks, but despite our attempts to keep watch individually, we've been unable to catch anyone in the act. For that matter, the only information we've been able to get at all is the occasional neighbor's half-remembered account of an older, brownish-colored car full of a bunch of suspicious looking teens.

The obvious solution, we decide, is to band together. Strength in numbers. We all fall in love with the idea of standing in unison against a common enemy. Not only will this be productive, this might even be fun.

We recruit as many as we can from the neighborhood and agree to meet at Henry's house. There are six adults in all, dressed in black and carrying whatever makeshift weapons we can find. With an old, forgotten Louisville Slugger from under Chuck's bed, Dan's slingshot, and my chipped and slightly bent samurai sword, we are completely unprepared. We are, however, 100% willing to go to war with a gang of street savvy thugs.

Over the next hour we discuss our plans. Who will cover which shift each night? What will we do if we actually catch someone? I've read enough comic books to get elected as leader, so I am the one forced to veto the most extreme game plans as they're presented.

"So if one of us can just catch 'em in action and chase 'em towards the others, we could hog tie 'em, gag 'em, and leave 'em layin' in the field overnight," Dan suggests. "The fire ants and the 'skeeters oughta do the rest."

"Let's try to come up with something … maybe a bit more legal," I say. Talking to him is like trying to explain to a child with Downs Syndrome why he can't have a balloon. And it's not just Dan; no one is really helping.

"So I guess pumping them full of arrows and hanging them from a tree like little ghetto-porcupine-piñatas is out of the question?" Chuck chimes in.

"You a damn fool, Chuck. You know that?" Henry laughs. "A damn fool." He French inhales his blunt, a reverse waterfall of smoke flows upwards into his nose.

"Seriously?" I reply.

When the meeting — if you can call it that — adjourns, the only decision we have come to is that we definitely need a place to mount our defense. We need a secure location. We need a fortress. I volunteer the tree next to my apartment, and suggest that we might be able to put some sort of platform halfway up. We begin construction the next day.

What starts as a 3' × 3' perch soon becomes much larger. The next day Dan brings home a truckload of grocery store pallets and landscaping timbers. We add each one to the rest and before long erect a two-story, 200-plus square foot citadel. Over the next few months I forget all about the ring of thieves and concentrate my efforts on increasing the size of the tree house. Two old couches are acquired, and we haul them up into the branches. Electricity is run from my back porch via extension cords. Chuck has an old TV we can drag up there when it isn't raining.

I fabricate a roof above the first level, leaving the second floor open to the sky, a perfect place to lie at night and watch the stars scroll by. I am 12 years old again, and oblivious to the fact that I have absolutely zero construction skills. I use 20 screws where one would suffice. This thing is never coming down. We build on and into the summer.

With all of our attention focused on the newly-erected wooden castle, the dark brown Oldsmobile that comes creeping down the street late one night almost goes unnoticed. I get a call from Henry, who just happens to be out late adjusting the tension on the makeshift zip line (because a treehouse is nothing without a zip line) we had installed a few days before.

"These fools are behind the building, man. You in?"

"I'll meet you outside. Two minutes."

The building directly across the street is empty, and has been since Hurricane Rita ravaged this area a year ago. There is no reason for anyone to be back there at all. It can only mean trouble. Despite Chuck and Dan's insistence that we attack, cooler heads prevail, and someone makes the case for calling the police. 20 minutes later a squad car comes cruising down the road. It pulls behind the building and we circle around the other side to watch the action, excited, certain that we are about to witness justice's swift hand slap someone in real time.

Two officers run up to the car across the dark parking lot. Their flashlights bounce along the rusted body and then one of the doors creaks open. Smoke pours from the inside of the vehicle and the flashlight beams become solid yellow rods as they shoot through the billowing clouds. My first thought is that something is actually on fire, and then the realization hits me that the occupants of that car are just really, really high. It looks like a scene from a Cheech and Chong film.

"Damn, son. I need to get me some 'a what they got," Henry says.

What minutes earlier had seemed to be an open-and-shut case turns swiftly and shockingly sideways. The five teenagers are taken from the car, searched, and then handed back their keys with instructions to leave and not return. As the beat-up Cutlass rattles away, the police car follows them, and seconds later both are gone.

"Are you motherfucking kidding me?" asks Henry.

We all stand there completely slack-jawed. Clearly the cops weren't in the mood to write up a report. Though we have no solid evidence, we are all convinced that this is the same group of kids that has lifted our car stereos and CD collections. As we stare at each other in silent disbelief something even more surprising happens; the brown car comes back.

It cruises down the street through the darkness like a battle-worn shark, brazenly pulling in the drive headed back behind the building.

Henry doesn't waste a second. He picks up Chuck's bat and starts out across the street. "Man, fuck a bunch of these motherfuckers, yo."

We are all now ready for war. As we turn the corner behind the building we can see one of the kids clearly retrieving something from the grass next to the car; most likely something tossed when the police arrived earlier. The teen sprints back to the car when he sees us coming. "Go, go, go!" he yells, and the car starts to back up as he dives inside.

There is a wicked crack as Henry's bat connects with the windshield. The driver can't seem to get the car in gear, and Henry follows up with two more shots. The passenger window shatters and there is an agonizing crunch as the hood caves in. "Damn, man! This is my Mama's car!" a voice from inside cries.

"Then your Mama better have insurance!" Henry yells back as a brake light explodes in a shower of sparks and glowing glass. There are a few more glancing blows before the terrified kid manages to shift, and then finally the car speeds off, leaving us standing victorious amongst the wreckage.

"Maybe we should finish this inside," I say, figuring the police are certain to return soon now that a somewhat violent crime has been committed. By us, the brave defenders of our apartment kingdom.

We don't even make it back across the street before the red and blue flashing lights round the corner. Chuck and Dan sprint for home and Henry tosses the bat into the bushes. The car rolls to a stop in front of the two of us.

"I don't suppose one of you fellas want to tell us what happened here, do you?" the officer asks as he steps out of the car.

Seldom have any of my encounters with law enforcement over the years been positive ones, so I have adopted a strategy for dealing with them. When confronted by the cops, I go into what I call "Nerdy White Kid" mode. My demeanor changes instantly.

"Do you wanna tell us what happened?" he repeats.

I move in, adopting a very clueless and scared persona. "We heard some sort of hullabaloo and came to investigate!"

I hear myself use "hullabaloo" in an actual sentence. The officer looks at me dubiously, but I don't break.

"Seriously! There was some sort of ruckus outside! Thank God you're here, Officer!"

Henry isn't so calm however. "That car came back, man. Why didn't you arrest those fools the first time?"

"What Henry means is —" I start to say.

"What I mean is, if y'all ain't gonna stop these motherfuckers from coming over here, then we will."

The cop replies, "Sir, you can't say the word 'motherfucker.'"

In a moment of complete idiocy, I say, "No Henry. Apparently this motherfucker is the only one that can say 'motherfucker.'"

What a car full of drugged-out kids couldn't do in 20 minutes, I do in two. The officer shoves me up against the car before I can even begin to explain the hypocrisy.

"That's it. Turn around, son, and put your hands behind your back," he says, pulling out his handcuffs.

I am laughing as he clicks them shut around my wrists. Not only am I amused by the sudden turn of events, but I am also incredibly curious how talking to my neighbor could be considered a threat or a crime. "What exactly did I do?"

"You were inciting a potential riot," is his reply, "Watch your head." I duck as I am placed in the backseat of the car. If that was a riot, I would hate to see how he'd handle a group of Irish soccer fans. The officer sends Henry on his way and then gets into the car. His partner turns to me as we pull off.

"And I suggest you keep it down back there," he says. "We'd hate to have to tack any more charges on."

I know that technically I am going to get a Disorderly Conduct charge, and I figure that if I am going to get one, I might as well earn it. My tongue takes on a life of its own, and I empty both barrels.

"Oh really? Because legally I don't think I have to be quiet at all. If you don't like it, let me out. Or you could just turn up the radio, Captain America. Your wife must be really proud of you by the way. Bringing down the scum of society! How scary it must be for you! Ooooh, does it feel good, Kojak? You solved the crime! Yippee ki yay, motherfucker! Oh wait, I can't say that word. I forgot. Motherfucker.

You know the last time you were out here, we pointed out a guy that had driven up in a stolen car and tried to break into my neighbor's truck. Then he ran from you guys and when you caught him he had a 14" screwdriver in his pocket. And what did you do? You let him go. I've seen the detectives on *Court TV* put a guy away for life based on a piece of lip DNA they pulled off of a half-eaten apple core they found in a dumpster two counties away from the crime scene, and you couldn't piece that mystery together? Yeah, you're on fire, Commando Rabbit.

Why doesn't FOX ever follow you guys around for *COPS*, huh? Maybe it's because you fucking suck. You ever think of that? Maybe it's because dragging a guy to jail for standing in his own neighborhood is just shitty television. What a hero. You're the worst policeman ever. I hope your little radar gun really does give you cancer. Are we there yet? I've gotta pee. Come on, man! Speed! We already know you're a hypocrite, what's it gonna hurt?"

I keep my face as close to the partition as possible, throwing each sentence directly at his ear as he drives. I am determined to earn every minute of my stay in a holding cell. When we arrive at the jail, the two officers can't get rid of me fast enough. The ride has put me in a heightened state of amusement. Already resigned to my fate, and the misdemeanor charge, I commit myself to making the most of the experience. No one is safe.

They ask a million questions when they book me in, all for what I can only assume is my "permanent record." Once I realize that no one is here to determine the veracity of my answers however, I begin to lie. Even the simplest question is an invitation to mislead.

The woman in charge sits in front of her keyboard. "Height?" she asks.

"Six-eleven," I answer with a straight face.

"No you're not," she says.

"If you already know then why are you asking me?"

She growls a bit and then continues, "Do you wear corrective lenses?"

"Nope."

"What color are your eyes?"

"Is that with or without the contacts?"

"You just said—"

"I was kidding. Next?"

"Occupation?"

And in all honesty, I want to answer her correctly. The thought of having "comedian" next to my name in a file somewhere kind of makes me happy. The Bullshit Train has left the station however. I can't stop. I contemplate my answer as she repeats the question. "Sir? Occupation?"

And with the most serious expression possible I reply.

"Dragonslayer."

I even arch my eyebrow mysteriously as I say it, as if that will somehow add authenticity to my claim.

"What?" she asks.

"Dragons. Large reptilian creatures. Did you not have a child-hood, lady?"

She cocks her head sideways, baffled. "And where do you do this?"

"Caves. Meadows. Wherever the need arises," I shoot back casually. "Y'all took my sword."

She still doesn't know how to process what I am giving her. She has a blank to fill in on a form and the words coming out of my face confuse her. "And … people give you money for this?" she tries.

"Sometimes money, sometimes a virgin or a goat. Whatever the village can afford. I have a calling, lady, and I won't stop until all the dragons are dead."

Eventually, especially once I know my friends have arrived with my bail money, I cooperate. I manage to keep a maniacal little smile the entire time though, which does a phenomenal job of keeping the other people in the holding cell convinced that I am at least a little bit insane.

"What are you in for?"

"Killing lizards," I snap.

The tree fort lasts longer than I thought it would. One day a letter arrives at my door from the landlord. Apparently a make-shift platform of 38 pallets suspended 15–20 feet in the air is an "insurance risk," and news of the tiki torch someone had drunkenly dropped on one of the couches has made its way back to her as well. It must come down, the letter says.

Getting it up had not been a problem. Getting it out of the tree proves to be a different story entirely. I pull on the beams, I hit things with a hammer, and I jump up and down. Nothing fazes it. "Damn, I'm good," I think to myself, then I tie a rope around one of the support struts and pull some more. I even go so far as to ask myself, "What Would Jesus Do?" Then I remember that Jesus was an actual carpenter. He could probably dismantle this entire thing in one afternoon with his Jesus powers.

Eventually I give up. It stands stoically in that empty lot for another two years after I move out. Even after my relationship ends, I still sneak back to visit it, hoping against hope that my ex won't be home when I do. Time ultimately takes its toll on the untreated lumber. Pieces fall one by one over the following months until, exhausted at last, the final section surrenders itself to the elements.

LEAVE NO TRACE

We pile into two vehicles, loaded down with supplies and towing a trailer full of canoes. Six of us are heading across the state of Texas to spend a week paddling through Boquillas Canyon, hopping across rocks, and sleeping under the stars.

It is an eclectic group. I am traveling with two former Boy Scouts, a pothead, his girlfriend, and a hippie-type named Allison. Allison is a friend of a friend. Formerly a waitress, she has just recently returned from a three-month stint living in a forest. "Oh cool," I say. "You stayed with a friend who has a house in the woods?"

"No. I actually lived in a forest," she replies.

"Like a squirrel?"

"No. Like a person, just without a house."

"So, like a squirrel." I'm confused.

I am now given the canned anarchist speech about the shackles of societal life and the evils of government in general. I start to comment, but am met with the glazed-over eyes of someone that clearly has no interest in a real conversation. "All I know is that I don't want to work anymore," she says. "I just want to go back and live in Florida with the rest of the Rainbow Family."

To be more specific, she means The Rainbow Family of Living Light. It's basically nothing more than a large group of homeless gypsies; think Burning Man without the burning man. In their own egalitarian way, they have removed any sense of lower, upper, and middle class and instead all just choose to live in poverty. They build tent cities in the middle of our national forests, filled with beggars and runaways and, amazingly enough, families with children.

"Children?" I ask.

"Yes," she says. "And some of the children were so bad. It was unbelievable. One time a six-year-old called me a 'fucking idiot.' At six!"

"Well, he *was* dragged into the woods to live with crazy people. I can see how he might have seen you that way. You're a grown woman who lives in a forest."

After ten hours on the road and a few hours of uncomfortable napping, we finally push the canoes into the current of the Rio Grande. Emery is the trip's leader. Emery was a Boy Scout for as long as they will let you be a Boy Scout and he's brought another formerly dedicated Scout friend with him. Though I have grown to love the outdoors in my adult life, I never did any of that type of thing in my youth and, while I have learned to keep myself alive in the outdoors over years of exploring, I know very little of the official protocol.

In Scouts they teach you a few core ideals. In addition to things like "doing your best" and "always being prepared" and making up mottos, Scouts are taught to leave no trace when exploring our nation's wilderness. This tradition was briefly mentioned to me before we left, and I agreed to it casually.

"It's a Leave No Trace trip," Emery said to me over drinks a few days earlier. "You cool with that?"

"Sure," I told him at the time, and I took another shot of Jameson. Even now, I only admit to agreeing because he keeps telling me that I did. Still, "no trace" sounds simple enough to me. We won't leave any trash. Yay, look. No trace.

What I have failed to grasp is that they intend to leave nothing whatsoever. Trash cannot be burned; it has to be packed out. If you have to pee, you have to walk 200 feet away from the river and find a spot devoid of plant life. Fires have to be contained, and the ashes brought with us when we leave. I can't imagine being in possession of a sack of ashes. "What's in the bag?" someone might ask.

"A phoenix," I will reply.

There can't be any leftover food either. If it is prepared, it must be eaten. I am already having difficulty on the first night. "I'm not eating your stupid fucking pudding, Emery!"

"You have to. We all have to do our part. Those are the rules."

"Those are your rules. I'm going to dump it in the river, Emery. I am. Watch me."

"Dude, that's not cool."

"No. What's not cool is making ten cups of vanilla pudding for six people that don't like fucking pudding. This is dumb."

"Give it to me then," Allison chimes in. "I'll eat some of it."

"Of course you will," I fire back. "You've been homeless for the last three months." We are not off to a good start. There are still four days ahead of us.

Boquillas Canyon cuts its way through Big Bend National Park, winding some 20 miles as it separates Texas from Mexico. As you approach the canyon, its walls tower ahead of you. The rocky ledges are home to mules and semi-wild horses, as well as what the guidebook refers to as "both friendly and not-so-friendly Mexicans." Yes, that is a direct quote.

The friendly Mexicans make our trip amazing. As our canoes drift along the lazy river current, all sorts of characters appear on the craggy cliff ledges. It is a very convincing recreation of Disney World's *Pirates of the Caribbean* ride, but with fewer drinking pirates and more drunk Mexicans. Instead of "yo ho ho" a man wrapped in a poncho sings "ay ay ay," and then peels off the next few verses of *Cielito Lindo*. The sun hovers unthreateningly in a brilliant blue sky and for a moment I forget that I want to drown the hippie girl.

The most wonderful part about camping for me has always been the sky at night. My fascination with the massive expanse of outer space is always amplified when I am removed from the constant glow of city lights. Here in the backcountry, the sky is just a high ceiling. I don't feel like I'm outside at all, but instead lying underneath some richly gilded canopy. The longer I stare at the sky, the more stars appear, and before long I am hypnotized.

After eating an entire gallon of lasagna against my will, I pull my bag out of my tent and find a secluded spot away from everyone in which to gaze out into infinity. At dusk the bats flit through the dimming sky, capturing the orange of the firelight on their wings and lighting up just briefly before fading away again. The water trickles and rushes off to one side of me and lulls me to sleep in the perfect night air.

Each morning finds us breaking down our campsite and piling everything back into the canoes. I am sharing paddling duties on mine with the other former Boy Scout, Walt. Walt proves to be an exceptional canoe mate and will eventually be my co-pilot on our trip back home, but he also possesses of a lot of completely useless knowledge. He creates crossword puzzles in his spare time and has thus come into contact with several thousand facts that he is more than happy to share with anyone who has ears.

When Allison turns down seconds after our meal tonight, she says, "I'm not used to eating this much. I usually eat like a bird."

Walt sees an opening. "You know, technically a bird can eat more than half its body weight in a single day due to its high rate of metabolism and the amount of energy it takes to fly. It would be more accurate to say you ate the weight of a bird instead of like a bird. Some birds—"

"Walt?" I say.

"Yeah?"

"Shut up, Walt."

We carry on like this the entire week. Emery prepares insane portions of food for the six of us and then continues to dump it onto our plates until it's gone. The only thing I will commit to consuming all of is the coffee. Walt can explain the food's origins. Allison thinks it would be better if we grew it organically like they did in the forest. "Well, we grew the mushrooms and the pot," she says. "We would beg or dumpster dive for the rest."

The other tag-along on our journey is Von, and Von brought his girlfriend Ashley. Von has brought — and this totally escapes my observation at the moment — a plastic container full of hash on the trip. His little foil pipe and Tupperware box make their appearance around the fire every night, unnoticed by me because I am too busy fighting with his girlfriend, who has chosen to stand in solidarity with Allison in their hatred for all things civilized. "Stupid fucking drug laws," she says. "We live in a country that is set up to keep us down, man. Pot is not dangerous at all but the government hasn't found a way to make money off of it yet so they keep it illegal. It's all run by corporations and I don't want to be part of it anymore. I'm not giving them shit for taxes anymore."

"What about things like schools and roads? You drive, right?" I ask.

"Only because I have to. There should be no laws at all, but the government should still have to take care of our basic needs," Ashley says.

"Are you actually listening to your own words?" I try.

"Whatever. I would happily live in the forest with you, Allison," says Von.

"You know there are some trees right over there," I say, pointing a mile off into the distance. "You two could go practice."

"You're such an asshole," Ashley says.

"I know. But you're a Communist."

Their desire to take more than they give weaves its way into our daily regimen. They are both conveniently absent when it comes time to break down our camp in the morning or to set it up at night. On the river they both sit in the front of their respective canoes and pretend to paddle, and still somehow find a way to point out that they think my canoe is lighter than theirs.

"He's not working as hard as us!" they yell across the water.

"What? How can I work less than zero?" I yell back. "It's impossible. I can't negative paddle. Even if I were paddling backwards, I would still be doing more work."

If Von weren't consistently high he might feel the need to defend her. As it stands though, I just fall into sync with Walt's paddling, and we drift out ahead and away from them. Walt's voice appears behind me, "You know that in the Bushi region of the Congo, women aren't even allowed to speak at all in public and for that matter —"

"Hey, Walt?"

"Yeah?"

"Shut up, Walt."

Despite my career standing in front of massive groups of people, I am not a social creature. I prefer isolation and time alone. I happily contribute my share to any group effort, but all in all, I am not a fan of communal living. I'm taking every chance I can to scramble off amongst the boulders and cliffs along the way, losing myself in the sand and shadow along the river's edge. It is cathartic and freeing, regardless of the tension between the girls and me on this trip. Night after night, a glimmering strip of sky hangs between the canyon walls, daring me to reach up and run my fingers through the starlight. It is remarkable.

We pack up the trucks after our last day in the backcountry. Loaded down with equipment and canoes, we begin the long trek home. We leave the river in immaculate condition, in some places even cleaner than when we had arrived. We were good little Scouts, all of us. No trace at all. Emery offers to drive first, and with Allison and Walt in the other vehicle, Von and Ashley climb in behind me.

"I really have to pee," I hear Ashley say, as I drift off to sleep in the passenger seat.

"Too late now," Emery tells her. "You'll have to wait until we stop."

Sometime later, I hear a voice I don't quite recognize. How long have I been asleep? I crack an eye open to see the fuzzy outline of a militant looking Border Patrol agent standing at the driver's side window. I pull myself up straight in my seat.

If Christoph Waltz's character from *Inglourious Basterds* had a Latin cousin, I've found him. Nothing is out of place on this man's uniform. It is spotless and polished, and he carries one leather glove that he rhythmically slaps against his open hand. His accent is thick and cocky, but he still looks like a cartoon Mexican Nazi.

"I need zee four of you to step out of zee vehicle," he says. We all comply, and then watch as Walt and Allison drive past us and on down the interstate. Certainly Walt is telling her all about the history of the United States border with Mexico, while she inquires about the right to live in the deserts on the other side of the Rio Grande.

"Zee reason I have detained you is because our dog has detected, how you say, zee smell of drugs in your vehicle. Now, we can do this zee easy way, or I can have my people take your entire car apart and go through all of zee contents until we find what we are looking for."

Ashley is doubled over as he speaks. "Sir, I really have to go to the bathroom."

"I'm sorry. You will have to wait until we have sorted ziss out." He smacks his glove and paces in front of us, trying to determine who is responsible. His apathy to her predicament is obvious.

So Ashley pees on herself.

The puddle widens at her feet while she stands as stoically as a girl covered in pee can.

"What exactly are you doing?" the Agent asks.

"I told you I had to go," she says.

"But zat is crazy, to just, how you say, go on your pants like zat?" As he speaks, I sit down on the ground. I am laughing uncontrollably. He smacks his glove again as he walks over to me. "Is it you? Are you on zee drugs? Is zat why you are laughing like zat?"

I am dying. I gasp for air and make seal noises as I try to find words. "She … I mean, I. No … you. Pee. Everywhere. Stop. I can't … breathe." I cackle like a maniac as I roll over onto my back.

"It's mine," Von says suddenly, possibly because his girlfriend is soaked in urine. "They didn't know anything about it." It is a respectable move, and the truth is that none of us did know that he'd carried his stash with him this whole time. I assumed he had finished it long ago, and even if he hadn't, that he would have been smart enough to ditch it before we arrived at a border check station.

"Well," says the Agent, "We will have to put you in, how you say, zee holding cell until we get zee sheriff on zee phone. Zee rest of you, come with me."

We are escorted into the station and held while they go through the car. Von sits in a cell in another room while Ashley, now in a fresh pair of clothes, continues to complain. "This is the problem, man. Stupid fucking laws like this. That's why I don't want to live here anymore. See?"

"I totally agree with you," I say. "This is a stupid law. But you know what else is stupid? Bringing drugs through a Border Patrol station. And guess what? The minute they let us go, I'm leaving him here."

"It was pretty dumb," Emery says, cutting his eyes at her. "And you peed on yourself. Don't forget about that. That was awesome."

We sit here for five hours while Von is taken to jail by the Sheriff and then we are released. With no cell phone service, we pull into the city of Marathon, Texas, proud population of 470. There is only one business open and it is a bar. Walt and Allison are sitting inside as we walk in. Apparently they have befriended the bar owner who has offered them dinner and arranged for them to stay at the bed and breakfast across the street.

"I think I might just stay here for good," says Allison. "They have an organic garden in town where I can grow things and there is a hostel where I can live."

"You're just going to move here after five hours?" I ask.

"I think so. Where's Von?"

Emery answers her. "We can't get him out until morning, so I guess we're just going to stay here until then."

I, however, am not. "I'm driving, Walt. Give me the keys."

"Shouldn't we—"

"Walt?"

"Shut up?"

"Thanks, bud."

It is almost midnight when I pull the trailer full of canoes away from the curb. Walt is asleep in the passenger seat, drunk and snoring, and as the lone light in Marathon fades behind us, I can't help but smile a little bit. Aside from dropping off a gypsy girl to live in West Texas, it really is like we were never there at all.

THEY WILL SEND ITS HEAD TO LITTLE ROCK

I arrive in Pine Bluff, Arkansas the same way I have arrived in so many other small towns over the last decade. There's a rhythm to it. I pull in. I check into my hotel. I lower my expectations. I tell jokes. It's really a short checklist. As I walk into the club for this weekend's shows however, a new bullet point forces itself into the mix.

Don't get rabies.

I enter to find the staff fully engrossed in the hunt. A cat — a gorgeous white cat — has crashed through the outer perimeter. The way they make it sound, you would think a terrorist operative was loose in the building. A pale flash shoots from under a table, followed by a blur of mullet and overalls.

"Sumbitch!" says the Mullet. "He's fast."

The rest of the team moves into place. The girl behind the bar tries to scare it into the back room while a 300 lb man with disturbingly saggy pants puts on his "plumbing gloves" and grabs a tablecloth. I stand at the far end of the bar laughing. Suddenly the Big Man lunges at something invisible. From under the bar, a hissing, snowy explosion shoots upward, landing on a rack of glasses and destroying half of them. The cat's screech melds with the sound of shattering glass as the Mullet leaps over the bar. Apparently cornered, the feline sits crouched on top of a Jagermeister machine, inches away from the liquor shelf. With its hair bristling in defiance, it dares either of the men to try to grab it.

The Big Man already has a plan. "I think … I can … get it," he starts to say. The cat hasn't had nearly as much to drink as the man has however. They move at the same time, the lumbering man knocking over the Jager machine and the cat knocking over every single bottle of alcohol on the top two shelves. In a beautiful cascade of falling glass and colorful liquid, it sprints towards freedom.

I am really pulling for the cat. I am. I don't consider myself a cat person by any means, but I did own two that I adored. They thought they were dogs and they were amazing pets. Athens was a huge animal by feline standards; huge and lazy, with a brilliant personality lurking beneath his layers of lethargy. Isabella was the smaller one, a gorgeous little white ball made of metabolism and cocaine. Cats were ideal pets for me because they could be left to take care of themselves for a few days at a time while I worked the road. In the comfort of my apartment, they were perfect. When I attempted to move them to Los Angeles with me, they were not.

2,000 miles from the east side of Texas to Los Angeles is not a difficult distance to cover when you travel as much as I do, but doing it with two cats? It's easier to convert to Hinduism, kill yourself, and hope you get reincarnated as someone that already lives on the West Coast.

There's no guide for how to transport cats. Dogs are simple. You put them in the car and pull over occasionally so they can go to the bathroom. Fish you can stick in a baggie. If I had a frog I could freeze it and defrost it when I got where I was going. If I had a dragon it could fly over my car and eat cattle along the way. There is, however, no simple way to get cats from one place to another.

So I got tranquilizers.

Veterinarians will sell you animal sedatives if you ask nicely enough. If you just go in and show them the feisty little creature you're attempting to transport, any vet's assistant will chuckle at your misfortune and then go grab a cylinder full of happy tablets from the back room. The problem is that they don't sell you a way to get them inside the cat. Children are supposed to eat vegetables, but just because you buy broccoli at the store doesn't necessarily mean the kid is going to eat it. I ended up left with a bottle of pills that existed outside of the cats, and cats that were determined to keep them there. All I could do was stare back and forth between the cats and the pills, and staring doesn't get much done.

Eventually I realized that if I held Izzy tight enough, if I grabbed her by the scruff of the neck, wedged my fingers into her mouth, and stuck the pill down the back of her throat, that I could possibly pull this off. It was a simple plan actually, if you happen to be an octopus.

I was told that since she was the smaller of the two I should start out by giving her half a pill and I did. Somewhere in the process though, it disappeared. I don't know if she swallowed it, or spit it out and I lost it. Either way, I couldn't take that chance, so I cracked another one in half. I'm not 100% certain how many times we repeated the process, but she had somewhere between half a pill and six. Either way, an hour later she was knocked out like me pretending to watch *The Notebook*.

Sedatives will get you through about ten hours with a cat, and that's about all I dared stretch it to on the first day. The second day, after force-feeding them a few more, I took off again. 12 delirious hours later found the three of us in Phoenix, and the two of them were pretty adamant that we were to go no further. Screams were flying out of the cat carriers in the backseat, along with fur and chicken bones. I don't even know where chicken bones came from. It was like I had captured a gremlin.

It also does a good job of explaining why I am unafraid of the wild animal these hillbillies are chasing around the bar in Pine Bluff.

As the Big Man topples forward and the shattered glass falls to the ground, the cat abruptly takes a turn in my direction. It rockets off the shelf, plants its back paws on the Mullet's head, and shoots through the air. It hits the ground in a full run, slides across the bar floor, bounces off the wall, and fires itself directly at me.

If you've never had an animal throw itself at your face, it's hard to say exactly how you will react. If you had asked me prior to this moment I would have told you that I would react just like a ninja should. I'd simply snatch it out of the air with one hand, grab it firmly by the back of the neck, and then make a little coin purse out of its skin. Seriously, how hard can it be?

If you ask me six seconds from now though, I will not say such a silly thing.

As the cat hurtles towards me with its claws out I throw my hands in front of my face. It hits with its talons drawn and latches onto my forearm as I scream like a kidnapped girl on an empty playground. When I try to remove it, it strikes. Like a cobra. Two gleaming incisors sink into my hand and wrist, driving down to the bone. Previously untouched nerves erupt, sending fiery tendrils of pain though my arm. As much as it hurts, the irony of being bitten by the only thing in the entire state with a full set of teeth is not lost on me. Why couldn't the cat be on meth like everyone else? The Mayor of this city could bite me, and at worst I would only be gummed to death. This cat though, it has a perfect set of fangs.

I fling the cat off of my arm and watch the blood shoot out of my hand. "Well sheee-it," says the Mullet. "We thought you was gone be the one to git 'em."

"Sorry?" I manage to say. The cat is now hiding somewhere in a storage closet trapped behind a closed door. The girl working the door calls Animal Control, as someone should have done to begin with instead of sanctioning this Feline Redneck Rodeo. Left to wait for the extraction team, I turn my attention to my wounds. The bartender slides a feeble attempt at medical supplies across the bar to me: a Band-Aid and a shot of Jack Daniels. I pour half of the shot on the holes in my hand and then drink the other half. I have just finished covering the injury when the bartender hands me the phone.

"Buffy wants to talk to you," she tells me. She looks scared.

Buffy is the owner of the bar. I don't have a lot of experience with people named Buffy, but the name conjures up negative emotions for some reason. As a matter of fact, my only real recollection of that name being used at all, in a non-vampire-slaying way, is when my great aunt used to call her dog. Her dog's name was Buffy, but Aunt Jewel was somewhere around 114 years old, and she pronounced it "Buff-eh." She didn't give it the long E sound it was supposed to have, and she would snap it at the poor dog in a gravelly voice that she had earned by smoking three packs of Marlboro Reds a day for ninety-eight years in a row.

"C'mere Buffeh!" she would growl, and then this poor beat up little black dog would come slinking into the room like some sort of villainous sidekick. So when the bartender hands me the phone and tells me it is Buffy, I immediately don't like her.

I pull up a barstool as I take the phone. "Um, hello?"

"Tell 'em you dint git bit."

My mind tries to process the words, to no avail. "Huh?'

"Them Animal Coppers. Tell 'em you dint git bit or they gon' lop its head off and send it to Little Rock fer testin'."

"Look Buffy," I say, "It's a little hard to hide when I have blood running down my arm and—"

"Nooooo! They gon' chop its head off forever! That cat dint do nuthin'. You're gon' be fine. Folks get bit all the time 'round here and don't nobody die of no rabies. They gon' put its head in a box and send it off, I'm tellin' you!"

It is like *Alice in Wonderland*, without the Alice and without the Wonderland. Just me and cats with teeth and crazy ladies yelling about chopped off heads.

I'll be honest; I don't know the first thing about how you handle a feral cat once it's been contained. I'm sure that if there is a legitimate concern that the animal has rabies or is infectious they will be forced to put it down. What I don't think is that the State of Arkansas runs around arbitrarily beheading cats. Euthanasia doesn't include hacking something's head off with a sword, or scissors, or whatever else Buffy thinks they do to something they capture. I'm pro animal under almost every circumstance. If I find out that the cat is going to be shoved into some homemade Southern guillotine I will be the first to step up and say something. I'm not, however, going to stand idly by and let them not run a test on a cat that just chewed on my forearm like a dog bone.

An Animal Control employee manages to slip a snare through the slightly cracked door as I sip my Jack and watch. They pull the cat from the back room hissing and screaming and flashing its claws at anything that comes close, yet they still somehow manage to get it into a box. The door girl is fired by Buffy for calling Animal Control in the first place, and then they start the comedy show. From the back of the room I watch as everyone acts like none of this has happened. A person has lost their job over this. Big Man and the Mullet have long since left. It is just me in the darkness. Well, me and my fear that I might slowly be turning into some sort of zombie-werecat.

The show ends, I struggle through a night of sleep in a back-woods hotel room, and now I am here, sitting in this hospital waiting room full of hard, turquoise furniture. The combination of the fluorescent lighting's cold glare and the blue-plastic covered chairs heightens my anxiety. This room bleeds unease. If solace was their intent they failed, whoever chose the decor. It is 3:30 in the afternoon on an overcast day in a not-so-affluent suburb, 64° and cloudy just like in that Pearl Jam video. Somewhere Jeremy is at home drawing pictures, and I am waiting to get shots that will hopefully prevent me from transforming into a rabid Arkansan.

A fat nurse walks out as I contemplate my existence. How did I get here? I may or may not have contracted rabies. I won't know for an hour or so. What I do know is that somewhere in Arkansas there is a horrible woman named Buffy who believes all cats die of decapitation at the hands of the animal cops. I know that, and that I'm never going back to Pine Bluff.

I'LL SHOW YOU
TO YOUR ROOM, SIR

Each city is different from the last. For every Pine Bluff, Arkansas, with its rabid cats and hillbilly bar owners, there is the extravagance of a Los Angeles or Miami. Most places, though, fall somewhere comfortably in between. Shreveport, Louisiana and I, for instance, have a love/hate relationship. I've been coming here for the better part of a decade and I never know what kind of mood this city will be in until I get here. There are good weeks and there are bad weeks. I met one of my best friends here and she and I proceeded to drink the town dry over the next five years while we talked of bigger things and wallowed in our inside jokes. Then I dated one of the managers of the comedy club and managed to get myself banned for a year or so after we inevitably broke up. There was also a fistfight with two guys in Muppet costumes under the bridge downtown. I've been tased at least three times in this city. It's just how things go in Shreveport.

If I were a salesman, I would tell you that show business is glamorous. If you have even an inkling of talent in any entertainment medium you should quit your job immediately and go out on the road. Every night is packed to the rafters with people who want to absorb your ideas and celebrate your art, and often times the people who were turned away at the door because the showroom was over capacity will wait outside just to shake your hand or have you bless their baby. It is first class airfare and limo rides and champagne in ice buckets and so many 22-year-old models to choose from that some nights just that choice by itself can be overwhelming.

From your perspective as an audience member, I can only imagine what we look like. You took your once-maybe-twice annual trip to the comedy club because you and your husband finally found a sitter and there weren't any movies playing that you could agree on. Your eyes are one pair out of 300 or 400 that look with hope at that brick wall and curtains waiting for this hero, nay, this Jesus-with-a-microphone, to steal you away from the real world for an hour or so. Then, from the front row you see him take the stage.

He is a lone warrior marching voluntarily to confront humanity's single biggest fear. Public speaking trumps death on the charts. Death! There are people on this planet who, given the choice, would rather cease to exist than face *one* time what this one person has chosen to do repeatedly for a living. Fearlessly he stands in front of you, weaving words into punchlines and punchlines into larger concepts and all of that into an hour-long show that leaves you with a belly full of laughter and hope for the future. His verbal crafts will be shared by you with your friends at the office tomorrow, though you will miserably screw up the timing and empty them of all nuance.

And when he is done it is back to the tour bus to finish the chore of choosing a model for the night, and then up to the penthouse suite at the nicest hotel in the city.

I am obligated by the Laws of Comedy to keep those myths alive, though nothing could be further from the truth.

When I first started playing Shreveport, all the comics stayed in a hotel, a Holiday Inn in the heart of downtown that was walking distance to the club. Even with a healthy buzz, you were never more than five minutes away from a safe place to crash. The last time I was here, I stayed in a Marriott on the Bossier City Boardwalk. It was clean and quiet, and I didn't have to share it with any of the supporting acts.

Those are the bookends on my time in Shreveport, however. In between, I have stayed in all sorts of places. Choosing accommodations for comedians is an arbitrary decision it seems. There is no standard; you are at the club owner's whim. Week by week, you don't really know how it's going to be handled until your plane lands and you get to the club. Not at my level anyway. Celebrities get to choose. I get to take what they offer, and some clubs treat you with respect and some treat you like their current wife's ex-husband. The good is great. When I tour with celebrity friends I stay just up the hallway from them in gorgeous boutique spots. The top of the comedic food chain is responsible for the myth that we all live like rockstars, and I have been fortunate enough to dip my toe in that heated pool more than once.

The other extreme is not so glamorous though. There are several club owners who don't put acts up at all. If you don't have a friend in town to stay with, you're on your own. I listened to one guy explain that it just wasn't in the budget, and he proceeded to lose four back-to-back, $100 hands of online poker as he talked. Another booker in Houston used to shave a few dollars by putting his comics in a room 40 minutes away from the club. Even further down the list is the "comedy condo."

The condo is an apartment some clubs rent for the performers to cut down the costs of procuring three hotel rooms every week. Generally there is a master bedroom, and one or two smaller rooms. The headliner is awarded the bigger room and his own bathroom, while the opening acts share the rest of the place. It's not always awful, although sometimes it is definitely awful. The owner of a string of clubs in Canada rents out fully furnished, high-rise apartments. The Toronto condo has hardwood floors and leather furniture and a sprawling balcony with a view of downtown. It's almost a vacation, but it's also not the norm.

Most weeks in a comedy condo are like hugely awkward episodes of *Big Brother*. Two or three guys tossed in a place together, regardless of chemistry. And it's even worse when it's co-ed. On a typical week, one guy smokes pot in the living room and watches old episodes of *Sanford and Son* while the other comic wades through the smoke and tells the emcee, who is sleeping on the couch because there isn't a third bedroom, to scoot over. Whataburger bags lie crumpled on the beat-up kitchen table. There is internet access if you're willing to sit huddled in a specific corner and leech off of the neighbor's unprotected WI-FI signal.

For a while in Tucson, the condo was one of the worst in the business. In fact, it was the worst place I've ever stayed in my life, and I've been to Third World Africa at least a dozen times. It's where Denzel stayed in *The Book of Eli*.

The club had gone so far as to lay down strips of plastic sheeting to provide a walkway, not to protect the carpet, but to protect the feet of anyone foolish enough to wander through the place barefoot. It was the kind of place you would think twice about holing up in for the night even in a post-Apocalyptic world. It was a place zombies would attack or Michael Jackson would have shot a video. Comedians used to spend their afternoons hanging out in the lobby of the fitness center next door, reading magazines, just to avoid being in the place during the light of day.

Shreveport has one of these condos now. I walk into the apartment on a Thursday to find that it is already occupied by one of the club's bouncers. My surprise is apparent when I see the 300 lb man with tattoos and a goatee sitting on the couch, wrapped in an LSU Snuggie, watching *Grease 2*. I literally think it is a joke. He extends his hand backwards and introduces himself. "Cactus," he says.

"Aloe vera," I say quickly. I think we were playing a game where we just name plants. "Your turn."

"No, that's my name," he says.

"Oh, sorry," I say back. "I mean, I'm not sorry that that's your name. I'm sorry that I ... just ... never mind. Please don't eat me."

The name Cactus isn't as memorable as you might think. I forget it several times over the following days, accidentally calling him Cracker, Taco, Backboard, and any other random noun with a "K" sound that pops into my head. As it turns out, Tractor lives here. He is the permanent occupant of the master bedroom and proudly announces that this is so. "So, where am I sleeping?" I ask.

"That's what the other rooms are for," he says, and goes back to watching Michelle Pfeiffer on the television. I wander back into the apartment with my bags to find my room, which, as the headliner, should be the next biggest room. Instead, the second bedroom is already occupied as well. My opening act for the week, Matt, has claimed it. He and I have worked together before. He is a veteran of the road. Certainly he wouldn't have taken my room on purpose, I think. He knows better.

Before I can ask, Matt walks out of the room followed by his fiancé. I am living in a fucking commune. "We got here last night and Cactus said—"

"Whatever." I leave him in mid-sentence as I carry my bag down the hall to the final bedroom, and push open the door to what I can only describe as "solitary confinement." A dim light flickers to life as I hit the switch, revealing a single, twin mattress in the center of the room. There is no dresser, mirror, or other furniture at all. And what if Cakepan sleepwalks? I wonder, inspecting the broken door handle. I tug on the light fixture to make sure it is sturdy enough to hang myself from later.

And this is the way it always is on the road. I can't complain because nobody really cares. There are 100 guys that will come in and take this week for less money and fall asleep happily on Ketchup's sofa. So you tough it out and go back to the apartment and watch from the patio while the neighbor unwraps Sudafed capsules. Maybe his meth lab won't blow up this week, you tell yourself optimistically.

But it's fun.

That's the attraction to it. As long as it's not permanent I can handle it. I can handle pretty much anything for a few days. Even Shreveport. This keeps me grounded. It seems unfair sometimes to collect a check for spending an hour or two onstage each night. That part is the fun part. It's the rest of the day spent living like a refugee that gets me. That's what they really owe me the check for.

For having to hide at a coffee shop in the morning so that Karaoke and his Snuggie don't ruin my vibe. For having to share a bathroom with the feature act and his fiancé. For being half crashed on the couch when the emcee stumbles in drunk with a pizza and the loud, fat girl from the front row. For having to catch a cab back to the room every night because the club owner is too busy to make the seven-minute drive, if the definition of "too busy" was "doing coke with one of his waitresses."

When I owned my club — Comedy, Texas in my hometown of Beaumont — I tried to be one of the good guys. The best thing a club owner can ever do is stay out of the talents' way. My partner in the club was a different story. I don't know why, but the only qualifications to own a comedy club seem to be "failed comedian with a penchant for cocaine." Lee couldn't have been more over-bearing, sidling up to every week's headliner, desperate for approval, cracking hack jokes as he hosted the show, and laying down more lines of powder than a Major League Baseball groundskeeper.

In hindsight it's surprising our club wasn't cleaner than it was. Those guys love to clean. And they love to talk. Imagine trying to steel yourself for the stage, mentally preparing to perform, while a cranked-up radio DJ chatters incessantly three inches from your ear. I watched my buddy Joey lose it one night when he was head-lining. "I gotta go on stage, cocksucka! Somebody tell Lee and that $20 booger he's got hanging out of his nose to leave me alone! Go jogging or something!" You get paid to deal with *those* guys, and there is always one of those guys.

You get paid for having to spend six days with the overweight, anti-American Canadian who refuses to wear anything but boxer shorts during the daytime. For staying in a condo that's three miles away from the closest fast food spot and not having a car. For being charged full price for drinks. For all the time spent mall-walking and sitting in movie theaters to kill a useless day in a boring town.

That's where I earn my money. It's not for the comedy.

I walk back out to the living room where Cactus is still flopped across the couch. "Are you fucking kidding me?" I ask.

"Don't look at me," he replies. "I have to live in this shithole too."

A THOUSAND
TINY GOBLIN SOLDIERS

I think I've mentioned that I've been punched in the face a lot. My mouth often makes promises that my body isn't quite prepared to defend but that my ego won't let me back out of either. I have a list a mile long of things I've done that I shouldn't have, and that list is only slightly longer than the one of stuff I still do that I shouldn't. None of the good stories have ever come from playing it safe. Not one, which is why I've always been so quick to leap into the fray haphazardly.

But those are the actions of the young and invincible, I tell myself. War should not be waged in the physical ways of my youth, but with intelligence and maturity now. A cleverly-crafted phrase,

I try to convince myself, is far more effective than a strong right cross.

And yet somehow, despite the best of intentions, I can't quite shake my former tendencies.

I am hanging out after a show late on a Saturday night with my regular opening act on the road, Sam, a big black guy with dreadlocks. Big. That's the only adjective I know to describe him. Not tall or fat, because he's neither really, but just big, like he's made out of concrete and gravity.

The clinking of ice signals that we are empty, and we order another round of James and Jack and get change for a five. He and I have had an ongoing competition for years now, feeding dollar after dollar into the mechanical punching bags that bars began installing once they realized that alcohol and testosterone are worth a fortune when combined.

Basically, for 50¢, a little leather bag drops from the machine and registers how hard you punch it. It is mindless fun and a matter of bragging rights amongst the guys. With a healthy buzz, I feed another buck into the machine and swing. As I connect, I hear a voice behind me say, "You hit like a bitch!"

I immediately turn around, and no one is there. I turn back around to swing again, and I am interrupted mid-stride by the same high pitched voice. "You gonna hit it harder this time? Bitch."

That's when I see him. Four-foot-tall on-the-button, here stands the most confident midget I have ever seen in my life, staring up at me, growling. Midgets growl, like little bobcats. I lean forward with my hands on my knees and I look down at him, squinting like I am trying to make out fine print.

"What, bitch?" he says, throwing his arms out to the side. There stubby limbs hang, taunting me. Beckoning me. Challenging me.

"You can't do that," Sam says to me, shaking his head.

"Can't what?"

"You can't beat up a midget, dude."

"You don't think I can beat up a midget?" I fire back, testosterone surging.

"That's not what I mean," he says. "I mean you can't fight him at all. If you win, you are the asshole that just beat up a midget, and," he pauses and cocks his head, "And if the *midget* wins?"

"Brilliant," I reply, suddenly happy to be saved from the embarrassment of beating up a midget. "So, what then?"

"Just don't stoop to his level."

"Did you seriously just say that?"

Sam laughs. "C'mon, man. Let's go."

As we turn for the door we push past the angry dwarf, who isn't as content to let things slide as we are. He shoves his tiny shoulder into my leg and starts pulling on my shirt tail.

"What?!" I yell down at him.

"You better leave before you get your ass kicked. Because —"

I can't even begin to guess what this little creature's explanation is going to be for how he plans to hurt me. I don't know his story. I don't know if he grew up on the wrong side of the rainbow, but his "because" seems to hang in the air forever. The only thing I can imagine is that he is going to pull back a curtain and reveal an entire midget army prepped for battle; a thousand tiny goblin soldiers poised to attack with spikes on the tips of their boots and their teeth filed into fangs, while David Bowie sings about a baby.

"Because why?" I ask.

"Because I'm in the UFC," the midget finally says.

I don't miss a beat. "There's a University for Fantasy Creatures?!"

He snarls at me and tries to crack his knuckles, and then snarls louder when he realizes that his hands won't touch.

Sam says, "Okay, *now* you can fight him!"

I lunge forward and he shoots for the door. I don't know if you know this or not, because few people do, but midgets are supernaturally fast, and they click when they run. *Click click click click click.* Like a beetle. *Click click click.* You can Google it. That is science.

"He's getting away!" I shout, and push my way through the crowd after him.

"Throw your shoe at it!" Sam yells to me.

"What?"

"Your shoe! You never saw *Leprechaun?*"

"Huh?"

"The movie? With Jennifer Aniston? Whatever. If you throw a shoe at a leprechaun, they have to stop and polish it."

Ridiculous, I think. I'm not going to beat this thing with mythology. I don't need rumor and folklore; I need fact. I have to find a way to do some real damage to this midget. I don't want to simply tackle him, because I know if you touch one you can catch whatever it is that makes them all tiny. Still, it doesn't look like I am going to have a choice.

We make it out through the front door to find the little elf clicking off and away down the sidewalk. Even with a head start, he's hopelessly outmatched. He needs three baby steps to match my one, and it only takes me a moment to catch him. As I draw near he turns around and growls at me, midget juice dripping from his fangs.

"Rawr!"

His claim to have a background in mixed martial arts is at least partially true. In MMA, when an attacker shoots in for a take-down, a standard defense maneuver is to "sprawl", or flatten out forward so that your legs can't be wrapped up and controlled. As I get to the little creature, he does just that, except I in no way actually attempt a take-down. I just sort of stand there and giggle while he dives forward and lands on his bulbous skull like a wee-ble wobble that doesn't make it all the way back up.

My gut tells me to jump up and land on his head because you get a free wish when you do that. I remember reading that on the internet somewhere. Then I remember how lopsided and mis-shapen midget heads can be and think better of it, lest I turn my ankle.

There's honestly not a lot you can do with a fallen midget. It's a sad truth, really. You can either stare as they try to pick themselves up, which is like watching an upside-down turtle struggle, or you can attack. It seems unfair to kick him so I dive on top, twisting his leg into an impossible lock. A leg lock might not sound that impressive, but consider first how hard it is to actually locate a midget's knee, and the degree of difficulty becomes much more apparent.

The bouncers arrive now and begin to pull me away, and I can only watch as the midget pops up off the ground like nothing had happened to him whatsoever. He growls in my face as I hang helplessly from the grip of the three muscle-ripped guys the club has wisely hired to squelch this exact sort of situation.

As I struggle with them, Sam, like the good best friend he is, appears out of the corner of nowhere, and he hits this midget so hard I expect candy to pop out. It is the single most vicious uppercut I have ever seen, connecting right underneath the hobbit's chin, easily lifting him eight feet up in the air. It is so hard, in fact, that he might actually stretch the midget out for a moment. I don't know what the legal limit is — we don't lay him across a cooler like a redfish or a salmon — but he sails into the air and lands with a thud.

"You killed it," I say to Sam.

And then, beyond all explanation, the midget pops right back up and runs off.

Click click click click click.

The only explanation is magic. Midgets can do magic. Sam's punch could have knocked an elephant unconscious. A 48" manchild couldn't have survived it, yet somehow he does. And as that mystical little man clickety-clacks off into the night, my only recourse, since I can no longer reach him physically, is to throw a final verbal blow.

"I hope—" I yell after him, "I hope you get eaten by an owl!"

Sam and I shake the dust off and make our way back inside. "I can't believe I let myself do that," I say.

"What? Get in a fight?" he asks.

"Yeah. I thought I was grown up enough to walk away from it."

"Well, look at it this way. At least your last shot wasn't a physical one. You gotta start somewhere."

"Baby steps, right? Maybe I'm growing up after all."

"Not even close," Sam says. "We did just beat up a midget."

"Shut up and give me a dollar," I say. "It's my turn."

THE JOKER AND THE THIEF

"I need you to feature for Dustin Diamond," my friend Rachel says. Rachel runs the comedy club in Shreveport, and she wouldn't call me if she didn't need me. It sounds like a nightmare, but the fun kind.

"So can you do the week?" she asks.

Dustin Diamond is best known as the child actor that played Screech on Saved by the Bell, and by best known for, I mean only known for. Well, that and the fact that he also leaked his own sex tape and stabbed a guy in a Wisconsin bar, if you're trying to fill up a magazine article. "He's going to be here that week and he's horrible. I need him to sell the tickets and then I need you to make the people not sorry that they bought them." It is sort of flattering I suppose. "He's going to suck, and maybe if you're funny in front of him people won't feel so completely ripped off."

Before this sounds like I am blowing my own little air horn as a comedian, you need to understand this: Screech is the worst comedian you've ever seen. Ever. Take bad comedy, cube it, and then double that. Sandy Hook was funnier than Dustin Diamond. What compounds the problem is that aside from being a brutally bad performer, Dustin is also known for being a notorious joke thief. In the world of standup, originality is everything. It's the sacred code. Take nothing, ever, from anyone. Our jokes are our children. That little fact automatically makes him my nemesis.

Still, Shreveport and I have our history. Screech may be a headache to deal with, I tell myself, but my shows will be good. "I guess I'll see you in two weeks then," I tell Rachel.

I arrive at the club for the first show of the week to find Dustin sequestered in a corner. I walk over to say hello while he ignores me and plays with his cell phone. "Look, bro," he says dismissively, "I'm not your friend, I'm not going to be your friend. Sorry. Jennifer handles everything. Go talk to her."

"What do you mean, talk to her? I was just trying to be nice, man," I say, and then walk off. We are working Wednesday through Sunday, so I have five days' worth of him to look forward to. Apparently though, I am going to get to talk to his wife whether I want to or not.

For anyone that recalls Dustin's character from the early 90s, anyone that remembers seeing that nerdy little kid with the hiked up pants, and the goofy grin, and the Jewish afro, anyone that ever thought to themselves, "That poor boy will never grow up and marry a hot chick," — you were all correct.

Dustin's wife's name is Jennifer, and she looks like nine ugly people all at once. She is built like the bottom half of an hourglass and her face is all mashed up, like she tried to board a Greyhound from the front. Before it stopped. And her personality makes her even more ugly.

She wastes no time in explaining to me exactly how things are going to be, and she speaks every word with the saliva-filled lisp of a cartoon elephant.

"So what kind of material do you do?" Jennifer spits.

"Umm, jokes." I'm not sure what she is getting at.

"What kind of jokes?"

"Funny ones."

"Like what?" she presses, but I'm not having it.

"Like, I start with a set up, and then once I've put that out there, I usually try to get around to a punchline of some sort, and then I put these things called tags at the end sometimes," I say. "I have no idea what you're asking me."

"Well, here's the thing," she explains with an elitist smirk. "Other comics have a tendency to watch Dustin's act on the first night and then go up and do his jokes in front of him the rest of the week, and I hate to have those people fired."

Guinness shoots out of my nose.   Did she just—? No. There's no way. "Wait a second," I say. "Are you … insinuating that *I* might steal one of *his* jokes?"

"It happens," she hisses.

"No, no. This is backward."

The hypocrisy is obtrusive. Her calling me joke thief on Screech's behalf is akin to Richard Simmons calling someone a cocksucker. It is a black fly in your chardonnay or some other Alanis Morissette lyric. It is the pot and the kettle and the dish and the spoon all packaged into one nice neat little fruit roll-up of irony, and it kind of pisses me off. Technically it isn't an accusation yet, as nothing has really happened, but it is a great indicator that a storm is on the horizon.

The first show goes as expected. I do a half hour in front of him, and then about a third of the way through his set people start walking out. "You are so much funnier than him!" they say as they file past me.

In all honesty, I hardly know anything about comedy at this point in my career. I am okay, but nothing more. I'm not that good; he is just sincerely that bad. To put it in perspective, if you go to a nice restaurant and they bring you a stale ham sandwich as an appetizer, you might not be too impressed. But, if they bring out your entrée and it is a big bucket of shit, then you will probably check to see if they can bring you another one of those suddenly-delicious sandwiches. That's what's happening here.

When I walk off stage the second night, Rachel meets me in the green room. "You're not going to believe this," she says. "Are you ready?"

"What was wrong with that?" I ask. "I did okay, right?"

"Jennifer said you did one of Screech's jokes and they want me to fire you."

I laugh at what has to be a joke. "Oh, shut up."

"I'm serious," she replies. "Don't worry, you're finishing the week obviously. I just want you to know." People continue to leave in droves as we talk.

On Friday night we are scheduled for two performances. Jennifer lumbers toward me before the first show with a hateful look on her face. "So you're still here?" she asks. I just smile. "That's okay. You won't be by the end of the night," she says, and waddles off.

For the third time that week, I finish my set and hang out in the lobby for the inevitable exodus of audience members. The people flee the disaster again, this time going so far as to try to warn the crowd that is eagerly waiting for the second show as they leave. Dustin storms to the back room after his failed set.

I can hear a conversation in the office growing heated as the second audience starts seating. I walk in, intending to watch from the perimeter, and instead find I am the center of the argument. "Fire him or we're leaving," Jennifer slurs as she points at me. She sounds like she has a wet dish towel in her mouth.

"He hasn't done anything wrong," Rachel says, defending me even as she nervously glances across the room at the misshapen caricature I drew of Jennifer on the whiteboard a half hour prior.

"He's doing Dustin's jokes," Jennifer fires back.

"Dustin's not even doing Dustin's jokes!" I interject. I can't keep quiet anymore. "He's doing Keith Alberstadt and Sam Kinison and—"

"Look," Rachel says. "Nobody is getting fired. Slade's not stealing any jokes, believe me. We'll just have to work this out some other way."

"Then we're done here," Jennifer replies. "C'mon Dustin." And with that, Screech stands up and follows her out the door like a puppy. She packs up his balls and goes home. He leaves 260 of his fans sitting in the showroom ten minutes before show time, people who have chosen to spend both their night and their money to see him perform. It is a terrible thing to do, especially considering that there are no other comedians in Shreveport to cover his time.

"Oh my God," Rachel says, stunned. "They really left. What are we going to do?"

"Start the show I guess? I'll do as much time as I can. Don't worry. It'll be fine," I say, a lie that we both need to believe at the moment. "And hey. Thanks for sticking up for me."

We start the show on time. The only other act on the bill is the Master of Ceremonies, a hip-hop radio DJ named Flow with long dreadlocks and no jokes. If it is my job to provide the comedy, it is his task to prepare the audience for the absence of their celebrity headliner, and he fails miserably.

"Dawg, I got this," he says. "I'm gonna explain it to them so that they as ready for you as they can be. Trust me, 'ite?"

"Okay," I say, and he confidently heads off to the stage.

"Yo yo yo, check it out," he says quickly behind the microphone. "Screech got sick as hell and had to go home, but you're gonna love this next mu'fucka. Give it up for Slade." That is my entire intro. No last name, no nothing.

The room becomes a roaring waterfall of conversation, everyone suddenly wondering what is going to happen. "Did we hear that right? Screech isn't here? Wait, what?" It is pandemonium and it is incessant, even as I walk on the stage.

You learn early as a comedian that you have to capture the audience instantly. As I grab the microphone, my only thought is to get my first joke out immediately. Win them over quickly, no matter what. My words, however, are lost in the cacophony, just another inaudible buzz in a room full of confused voices. I desperately need to change tactics.

I flag down a waitress and order a round — a beer and a shot of Jameson — and then I sit down on the barstool on stage and gaze out at the chaos. My drinks arrive and still I sit on stage, unmoving. Eventually the spectators grow curious, ending their conversations and slowly staring back at me. At least they're paying attention now, I think to myself. I shoot my whiskey and stand up.

"So, I know you're wondering what's going on," I tell them. "I'm guessing you've figured out that Screech isn't going to make it tonight, and I'm sorry. That's the bad news. The good news is that you're much better off without him. You would only have been disappointed.

"I know Flow told you he got sick but that's not entirely true, and I think you guys deserve the truth. He walked out on you. He knew you were here and he chose to run off. He's a dick."

"Why'd he leave?" a voice yells out of the darkness.

"Honestly? He was doing that badly. He got embarrassed and he quit," I reply.

A different voice arises from the back. "You're lying!"

"Um, no. I'm not. He really did get embarrassed and he left."

"You're making that up!" the man repeats, louder.

"Why would you say that?" I ask, becoming a little defensive. "That's exactly what happened."

The response that comes back is one of the funniest things I'd ever heard in my life. "Because if ten years on *Saved by the Bell* didn't embarrass that motherfucker, then nothing could!"

It is met with uproarious laughter. "Fuck Screech!" he says. "Tell some jokes!"

And on that note, the crowd and I bond. I make it through the show unscathed, and no one leaves upset. It is a far longer show than I am capable of at this point in my career, but we all somehow get through it anyway. I haven't crossed paths with Screech since then, but I have occasionally run into a comic who has. "God, he's such an asshole," they say. "Have you ever worked with him?"

I always reply, "Let me tell you about this one time in Shreveport."

OCEAN'S BANANA

Texas is vast. It is a sprawled out, multi-faceted, cocky piece of real estate. That Texas swagger surfaces early, too, particularly if you've ever entered the state from the east. A bright green sign proudly displays the distance to other cities. Orange, Texas is four miles away and El Paso is 857, just in case you thought it was going to be a quick sprint from Louisiana to New Mexico.

"Howdy," says Texas. "This ain't Rhode Island."

As a comedian I have traveled the entire state. Literally, border to border to border to border. There are very few cities that I haven't heard of. We have Athens, Paris, London, and Moscow. There is a Venus, Earth, and a Mars, Texas. There is also a Cut 'N Shoot, Ding Dong, and Hoop and Holler. There don't seem to be too many rules when it comes to naming places here.

Tiny towns — villages really — dot the landscape, often little more than single traffic lights and a corner store set up to service the surrounding farms. There are mid-sized cities too, with their Walmarts and community colleges, and there are larger ones yet, with real universities and more than one intersecting highway. Then there are the Big Three. Houston, Austin, and Dallas. And all three pretty much hate each other.

The three cities couldn't differ more. Houston is gritty and a little dirty, more Mexican than American it seems sometimes, like a Latino Darth Vader. Dallas is shiny and pretentious, a rich but overweight cheerleader that nobody thinks is hot but her. Then there's Austin, immaculate because the hippies keep it that way.

The comedy scenes are quite different as well. Houston was home to Bill Hicks, Sam Kinison, Brett Butler, Janeane Garofalo, Thea Vidale, and the legendary Outlaw Comics. Austin arrested Mitch Hedburg. Dallas, well, Dallas has never really done anything at all.

I am among the group of comics that are setting off this morning for a down-and-dirty Houston themed one-nighter at Austin's flagship comedy club. Johnny, Rob, Andy and I drive limply onto the freeway around noon, a painfully early hour for people who do this sort of thing for a living. Every one of us is a veteran comic, but none like Andy. Andy is in his mid 60s now. He was one of the original Outlaw Comics and has been doing comedy almost as long as the other three of us combined. As we drive toward Austin, he tells story after story and we gleefully listen to them all.

"So Kevin Spacey falls down some stairs coming out of this gay bar late one night in England," Andy says. His way of saying it is so matter-of-fact that you instantly trust it, even if you can't confirm the source. This is also way before Spacey came out in an attempt to use his sexual orientation as a get-out-of-jail-free card. "People are snapping pictures of the injury and he knows it's going to be all over the news. He doesn't like to discuss his sexuality publicly, so instantly he gets on the phone with his publicist and they concoct this whole story about how he was out walking his dog and slipped and fell. I mean, sure, it was three o'clock in the morning, but he loves his dog that much. That would be the story they decided. People would buy that.

"So they set up this huge press conference for early in the morning so he can get in front of the controversy and explain that he was just out taking care of his furry little best friend. Then Spacey calls his assistant. Turns out his assistant at the time used to work for Madonna and Guy Ritchie, so this was barely on the radar for weird shit that he's had to deal with, but still, it's the middle of the night. The assistant answered the phone all sleepy, and Spacey said …" Andy paused for a second, giving it that flawless half-step that comes from 30 years of comedy.

"I'm going to need you to go buy me a dog."

And so this trip goes, four comics riffing in a car together all the way up Highway 71 and through La Grange. After our show, Andy retires to the hotel, his hell-raising days behind him, while Johnny, Rob, and I duck out with some people from the audience to finish off the night. Our friend Mike knows a bar a block from the comedy club, and we end up on the patio with some Austin locals.

Ninety percent of the 18–34 year old, male demographic in Austin looks exactly alike. Striped V-neck tee (or a not striped, but with a picture of Che Guevara or a Nintendo controller), glasses (regardless of whether or not their vision is bad), knit cap (despite being summer in Texas), and those god-awful skinny jeans.

I happen to be sitting next to their leader, who has replaced his Chris Martin-esque hat with a pair of sunglasses at 1:45 in the morning. "I had them on when I got here, man," he says, which means he had to have gotten here at 7:00, which means he is either lying or that he has been at a completely dead bar for seven hours, which means that either way he is probably a complete loser. As if to confirm my suspicions, he slides a business card across the table that has the words "The Poet of Funk" printed across a picture of him combing his hair while wearing his signature sunglasses.

"I do alternative hip-hop," he says.

"I don't know how to talk to you," I reply, and turn back around to my friends.

Rob is talking to the girl that runs the bar's karaoke night, or rather is talking directly to her boobs, and Johnny is engrossed in another conversation, and next to them sits an eight-foot-tall stuffed banana with a huge smiling face and dreadlocks. Johnny isn't a small guy, but this massive fruit dwarfs him. I blink a few disbelieving blinks, and when I open my eyes again it is still there.

I glance around for an explanation, but a round of shots comes out before I can ask.

"That's our mascot," the bartender says as he set the drinks down. "The Rasta Banana."

"That's some real shit, right there," the Poet echoes, sipping his Pabst Blue Ribbon. "It's 'dope' than a motherfucker."

And I know at this exact moment there is no way we are leaving without stealing that banana.

A heist is a difficult thing to orchestrate, especially if you've never orchestrated a heist before. Every plan that begins to form dissolves just as quickly. I am the Danny Ocean of the group, and I need things if we are going to get away with something this big — things like a helicopter, a flatbed truck, and Daniel Craig — and we have none of those things. "Gimme your keys," I say to Mike.

"Why? You're not driving my car."

"Of course not. I just want to, um, look at them."

"Oh," he says, and then flips me his keys. "Ok."

It doesn't matter that there is no way the banana is going to fit in his car with the rest of us. That is a math problem. I dropped out of college so that I wouldn't have to do math, and I'm not about to take it back up again. Getting it in the car is not my responsibility though. I have bigger problems. The patio is still full of faux-beatnik kids and bar employees, and someone has to get them inside. I slip the key to Johnny and whisper some quick instructions. He and Mike are going to be the extraction team.

Rob's job is the girl. I text him from across the patio, and he glances up at me to let me know he's gotten the message. *Get karaoke chick out of here.* He stands up, says a few words, and she instantly heads out into the parking lot with him. We won't see him again until the next morning, and I am amazed at his efficiency. No one has told him about the plan to steal the banana. He just follows the order unquestioningly, like a Secret Service agent or one of Caesar Milan's dogs. It is perfect. I can't imagine what he said to her, but whatever it was, it worked.

"Hey!" I yell suddenly to the remaining few hipsters. "Shots on me at the bar. You can tell me about your dope ass hip-hop," I say, and three skinny vegan rappers follow me inside. Positioned strategically at the bar, I order four well whiskeys straight. It is rot gut stuff that no one drinks without a mixer, but I need the extra time that their reaction will buy us.

I glance over their shoulders as they look hesitantly at their shot glasses. The banana is slowly moving across the patio toward the exit. Maneuvered from behind by Johnny, it jumps another jerky foot every second or so, like a big, yellow, stop-motion Gumby, and then suddenly it is gone, tucked miraculously into the back of Mike's vehicle. I drop $20 on the bar. "Enjoy the shots!"

"Yo, check me out on Facebook!" the Poet tries. I am already out the door.

We descend on Mike's house like a swarm of drunken bees, each one of us recanting our part of the heist, toasting the banana, and flopping down on top of it like it is some huge, yellow Santa Claus. It moves from the kitchen, to the living room, to the back patio, finally free of its counter-culture captors and in the company of (in our minds, anyway) giants. I can't tell you how many pictures we take both of and with the banana, but I know that it is more than one, and that is still too many.

The next morning finds us completely puzzled as to what to do with it. Andy just shakes his head, happy that he chose to retire for the night. "Not even in my younger days," he says, though we know that's not true. Rob isn't exactly sold on the idea of tying it to the top of his car for the three hour trip back Houston, so we finally decide that we should just return it. Not a creative return like in *The Thomas Crown Affair*, where we paint it to look like a Golden Tee machine, sneak it back into the bar, and then set off the sprinkler system, but a simple delivery of the mascot back to its rightful owners with an apology.

"We can't brag about stealing it if we don't return it first," Johnny says, and we all agree. It was never about keeping it anyway, we realize. This was a fraternity stunt, and we are a fraternity of sorts. It is one that goes back generations, comedians roaming the countryside, telling old stories while creating new ones, and there's not a stunt worth pulling if we can't talk about it later. As enticing as the thought of a bar full of hipsters crying over their loss is, a good tale is always worth more to a comedian than any stuffed banana, eight-foot-tall and Jamaican or not.

STYROFOAM GRENADES

Some mornings I wake up angry. I can't explain why or even what it is I'm mad at. I just know that it happens. Psychologically I'm sure it means that I am unhappy with some aspect of my life and that it is manifesting itself in my mood when I begin my day. I'm not a scientist though, and to be honest, I don't really care about why it happens. All I want to do on those days is shake the feeling before I inadvertently pass it on and screw up someone else's day by being a dick.

This is one of those days. I'm cruising down a Houston side-street and sucking down a grape slush from Sonic. They're my cat-nip. They remind me of ballpark snow cones but better, the way they would have tasted if that pompous concession stand lady would have given me extra purple juice like I asked for instead of trying to charge me 25¢ that I didn't have. Usually one of these slushes does the trick, purging that occasional morning anger from my system, and tapping it out quietly so that I can go about my day unhindered.

I round the corner less than a mile from my house. Washington Avenue merges with Hempstead Road, the two becoming a single, crowded, one-way street in a matter of 100 feet or so. As I settle into the new lane, a silver suv appears in my rear view mirror. It rides up on my bumper, lurches left, accelerates, swerves violently back in front of me, and continues to do the same thing to the next two cars in front of him like a pissed off little checker. His silhouette betrays the fact that he is not simply driving like an asshole, but that he is on his cell phone as well. Like an asshole.

My gut screams at me to follow him, to cut him back off and then slow him to a crawl, but I take another swig from my slush and make myself breathe deeply.

I have calmed down significantly as a driver over the years. I've driven aggressively and fast since the moment I turned 16, like I'm piloting a spaceship into battle. I got three tickets in one day driving across Texas to a gig — one in Sour Lake, one in Conroe, and one somewhere in Palmer County. I also showed up in Dallas that same trip with only one shoe, having flung the other at another driver that kept me stuck behind an 18-wheeler for several miles. I'm not proud of it.

I drive fast and mad. It's not road rage per se, because the frustration continues long after I've gotten out of my car. Little things irk me throughout even the most regular day. I hate that we are subjected to a world that thinks we're stupid. I mean, there are billions and billions of stupid people, but not *us*. We're the exceptions right? Pre-recorded commercials run on television with countdowns on them. *Call now before time runs out!* Who believes that? Obviously someone. Infomercials talk to me as if I have a disability. *Has this ever happened to you?* And then some palsied grandmother spills spaghetti all over her face and the kitchen. No. It's never happened to me. I can drain pasta just fine. My muscles tense when these people try to sell me things. I want to hit something, just to make them stop shoving this crap in our ears.

Back on the road I tap my foot at every two-in-the-morning red light. I can't rationalize in my brain how there are no cars for miles, yet I have to stop and wait until some mechanical gatekeeper grants me permission to go. I don't need a babysitter to operate a vehicle. It makes me want to rip the wheel from the steering column. Traffic stops for no reason and then starts right back up again. Why? No one knows. So no, it's not road rage, because it's not the road that makes me mad. It's all of the things on the road.

I have a total lack of compassion for inferior drivers. Turn off your blinker after you've changed lanes. Don't get in front of me. The speed limit is not 22 mph anywhere. Seriously. This isn't a school zone. Have you ever driven a car before? Sweet holy Christ with a cutlass! I wish I could make your car explode with my mind. Pull out in front of me. I dare you. I am fully insured …

Okay. Maybe it is road rage.

But if it is, I blame my grandfather for at least part of it. I have vivid memories of being driven to school in the fifth grade, of being told to hold the wheel of his 30-foot-long, bright copper, 1979 Mercury Cougar so that he could lean out the window and curse other drivers in Arabic. He was amazing. All of that is my past though. Sure, I still get angry when I drive, but I don't act on it. I've tried to do a much better job over the last few years of attempting to understand people's motivations for the ridiculous things they do. I honestly try to be more compassionate because you never know what's pushed a person to behave in a certain way.

So when this shiny Escalade comes barreling by me and forces me to slam on the brakes, ruining my perfect grape-slush-and-Led-Zeppelin vibe, I have to wrestle my first instinct. Certainly this guy has an emergency. What if something happened to his daughter and he is rushing to see if she's okay. I don't want to interfere with that. Maybe someone broke into his house and he is on the phone with the alarm company. Have sympathy for him instead of animosity, Slade. He's just regular guy having a ba—

Did that fat sonofabitch just pull into McDonald's?

That is the emergency? My foot presses down on the accelerator, subconsciously, despite my mind's attempt to play peacekeeper. Breathe, it says. Whatever, my body says back. I shoot around two cars of my own, back and forth, until I have secured the inside lane that runs parallel to the drive through window.

And that's how I lose my slush. Left-handed and a little side-armed, my half-filled, purple, Styrofoam grenade rockets out of the open window toward the idling suv. I don't see the impact but

I'm pretty sure it connects; I had plenty of time to take the shot and he was a stationary target. I round the curve just after the release but I hear a car horn blare loudly for several seconds as I make the arc. I know it was him and it makes me smile.

It's contagious, that hostility. I caught it from him, and he certainly caught it from somebody else. I fell into the pattern of passing all that negativity along by accident. I attempt to be conscious of this kind of thing, because I know it really only takes one person to interrupt the cycle instead of perpetuating it. Next time, I intend to be less reactive. Next time I will do the positive thing and simply side-step all of that bad energy.

But that's next time. This time I fucking nailed it.

SILENT WARRIOR

Sometimes a comic has a bad set for a reason you could never possibly know. Maybe it's a family problem running amok in the back of their mind or maybe it's a day of dealing with car trouble, but for whatever the reason their head is just not in the game. And sometimes that reason is lack of sleep.

It started at 3:00 AM and it hasn't stopped. It is relentless. It's the second attack in as many days and my sanity may suffer for it. I am under siege by the most well-trained mosquito assassin on the planet.

I have forever been aware of the buzzing annoyance that accompanies most mosquitoes. My springs and summers have been plagued by clouds of mosquitoes for as long as I can remember. This one though, this one is a special breed. A regular attacker can be isolated it by its sound. You listen to it as it gets closer and closer, and then slap the last place you heard it. I've killed them by the hundreds over my lifetime, and I'm afraid that's why they've sent this demon warrior after me. The Uruk-Hai of the insect world.

If you're confused, let me explain. This satanic little bug doesn't buzz. There is no warning, no tickle of the ear, no sudden silence to notify an imminent sting. Just the feeling of her tongue or beak or whatever it is as it punctures your flesh.

1,000 times in a single night.

I've read *The Art of War*. I know how the strategies of combat work. Sun Tzu says to know your enemy and I do. I know they're attracted to white and things that expel carbon dioxide. I know I am both of those. I'm a target. We are natural adversaries. It knows how to prey on me; I must learn how to prey on it.

But how do you fight something you cannot see?

This female ninja warrior trained in guerrilla warfare is unbeatable. From out of the darkness she comes, and, unrelenting in her hatred for me, tactically locates pieces of skin that extend past the protection of the hotel comforter. The comforter is usually the first thing I fling to the floor when I check into a hotel – I've never been convinced that hotels wash them – but now it is my last true layer of defense. I feel the sting and I tighten the muscle where she jabs me, hoping to somehow capture the proboscis in my arm and smash the mischievous little sprite into a puddle of her thorax and my own blood.

But she's gone again.

I drift back to sleep, another fitful 20 minutes before the next salvo comes. Is there more than one? There must be. If she's a lone wolf, she should be huge. She's had over a pint of my blood. Lie in wait. Feel the sting. Turn on the light and look for the thing that's the size of a softball. She's not there. She hasn't flown up to the light or landed on the wall like a typical soldier. She is simply gone, vampiric in her tendencies to bite and then fade into the night.

Am I going to turn into a mosquito now? I can't see her, I can't fight her, and I certainly don't want to become her. My only resort is to cocoon myself in the covers leaving nothing exposed. It's hot and uncomfortable but it will prevent further damage. Wrap up, tend to my wounds, and reassess the battle in the morning. She has to sleep sometime. I will be safe in my—

Ouch!

Are you kidding me? How did she do that? I just got stung again. Sweet Christmas, she's in here with me. That, or her stinger is long enough to penetrate this blanket. Oh my God, what if it is? What if I'm really up against some vampire bird with a foot-long pike and a cloaking device? I am not going out like this.

Covers off, lights on, I roll out of bed and hit the floor, fists up. Let's do this, motherfucker.

And just like that, she's gone again.

Am I crazy? No, the marks are still there. Aren't they? It's seven o'clock in the morning now. Maybe this is the product of my delirium. Maybe there's no mosquito at all. How ridiculous am I being? There are no non-buzzing mosquitoes. I'm just tired. Go back to bed. Stop hallucinating.

Of course, the greatest trick the devil ever pulled was convincing the world she did not exist.

And that is how she beats you.

THE DEVIL THUMBS A RIDE

There's no such thing as ghosts. Dorothy's mantra as she tiptoed through the forest sums up me perfectly. Despite what other people swear to be true, I don't believe in the physical presence of any of it. I'm a hard one to convince mainly because the only evidence I've ever been confronted with has been pure hearsay. Don't tell me a story, show me proof. Ghosts, demons, evil spirits; I am simply unafraid. That sounds like a blanket statement full of machismo and pseudo-bravery, but it's one of the few things I feel very confident about saying I'm not afraid of. I've made that very same statement in the past about several things, from heights to snakes, and yet if you put me on a roof with a cobra I would very likely cry like a little girl right before I pass out. I am not, however, afraid of running into ghosts.

The myth is that these spirits only visit those that believe. Certainly that could explain my total absence of other-worldly contact. Regardless of the reason, I have been in situations where I absolutely should have seen ghosts if there really were any to be seen. My first year in the comedy industry was spent bartending at a supposedly-haunted club. The building's history was somewhat suspect. What I knew for certain was that GK's Comedy Club was a bank before it was a comedy club and an insurance agency before that. If you listened to people talk, you could also tack Indian burial ground, mental asylum, and children's slaughterhouse onto its list of former uses. When I first started working there I was briefed. Tony owned the club and he laughed as he filled me in. "All the waitresses think there are ghosts in the building," he said. "If anything strange happens, just ignore it. Just between you and me though, these bitches are crazy."

Tony was ex-Navy, which somehow validated him in my mind, so his lighthearted dismissal was enough to make me forget about it entirely. The girls on staff wouldn't let go of it as easily though. Over the course of a few months, I went quickly from bartender to manager as Tony and his family moved a few hundred miles back to Austin. I was in charge now, of both the club and the staff of occult-fascinated waitresses. The stories they told came in faster and faster once he left. I had to be at the club almost the entire time it was open because the girls were too afraid to stay there by themselves. My army of cocktail servers seemed to be on one collective acid trip. One day it was shadowy figures walking outside past the windows. Another day one of them ran screaming from the restroom swearing that she saw a little girl sitting cross-legged on the counter an hour after we closed. "I'm not making it up," she said. "She was right there!" These specters mysteriously never hung around long enough for me to see them, and I found the staff's insistence maddening.

I ended up by myself in the club many nights. After the girls had left, I would pour a glass of whiskey and enjoy a brief moment of silence, sipping away the evening's drunken customers and inventory problems. As I stared into the darkened showroom, I would try to imagine the disembodied voices and shimmering shapes that had kept all my employees spooked. My ego started to toy with me. While I was reluctant to admit it, I did feel a little left out of the poltergeist house party. I eventually even started doing little things to invite their presence. I left lights turned off, and I intentionally stumbled through the blackness, falsely convinced that these phantoms would like me more if I kept it dark. Counting money at the bar alone at one o'clock in the morning, the walls would shift and settle, making groaning noises and prompting a response from me. "Is that you, Ghost Person? Come out and play! I don't believe in you, you know?" It was absurd. I was a grown man yelling into an empty room, feeling hurt that something I didn't believe in was ignoring me.

I ended up owning the club a year later, spending almost seven years there in all, each year passing without an encounter. When the club closed, I walked away chuckling at the scores of people that had truly accepted the building as haunted. Such fools, I thought to myself. No rational person could truly believe in the existence of ghosts. I adopted the official label of Skeptic and moved on with my life.

I'm at my brother Jeremy's house today. He is far and away the most logical and well-grounded of my siblings, and when he pulls me to the side I have no idea what he wants. As we stand in the driveway he lights up a cigarette and then gets very quiet for a second. "If I tell you something, will you promise not to think I'm crazy?" he asks hesitantly.

"Absolutely," I reply.

"I think I'm hearing demons," he states with a poker player's face. He is so serious that my mind immediately takes it in and processes it as fact.

"Oh wow, that's rare." I say it quickly, followed instantly by, "Wait, what?" Normal people don't hear demons. For that matter, even crazy people don't hear demons. They just think they do. He tells me, however, that every time he passes by a certain stretch of woods leaving his house he hears a deep, guttural voice whispering things to him.

"It's probably not a demon but it sure sounds like one. And it's an actual voice, too, not like some engine sound or anything. I'll figure it out," he says dismissively. "I mean, it's just a demon." Then abruptly, he changes the subject. "So I have Astros tickets tomorrow if you want to go."

Sometimes certain things leave our memories. We don't hang on to particular conversations for whatever reason, and somewhere down the line that negligence bites us. That conversation is one of those. In my mind there is no reason to give it any more credit than I already had. Demons aren't real either. They're just biblical ghosts, right? And, as I may have mentioned before, I don't believe in ghosts.

Every time I see one of those documentary shows about ghost hunters, I can't help but laugh. Watching adults run through abandoned hospitals and lighthouses in search of spirits trapped in them is the highest caliber of comedy. The fact that these people take themselves seriously is astounding to me. Light reflected off of dust in photographs must be an "orb." Any sound captured on a $10 Radio Shack voice recorder must be a message from the other side. Kkkkkkkkkccccchhhhhh. "Did you hear that? It said *GET OUT.* Seriously, did you hear it? Oh my God. That's insane! I'm so scared."

Those people are idiots, suckered into having to produce some results so that they can keep their made-up television show on the air. Everything is evidence, no matter how mundane. Certainly it can't be explained away by conventional means. In the world of the paranormal investigator, lights flicker on and off and doors slam shut without explanation. They're ghosts, they say. Electrical shorts and gravity would make too much sense. It must be super-natural when all of their batteries die at the exact same moment and not the result of having charged them all at the same time. I watch these shows with my skeptic's mind. These poor people are so easily swayed.

A few weeks after my conversation with my brother, I find myself hurrying out to my car, late for some unimportant thing or another, and accidentally without my ever-present iPod. It is during this incredibly rare moment of radio silence that I distinctly hear a voice whisper something to me in my ear. It is enough to make me skid to a stop in the middle of the road and look around. Still, logic is my friend. I write it off as some random sound, certainly coming from something that I drove past. Pull it together, I tell myself.

The next day I am driving again and have just gotten off the phone when I hear the same whispering voice say, "I'm going to kill you in your dreams." And this time it is very clear. "I'm going to kill you," it said. "In your dreams."

I double-check the radio settings to make sure I'm not hearing Sean Hannity by accident. I pull out my phone and make sure it is on vibrate. This is ridiculous. I don't believe in ghosts, I don't believe in ghosts, I don't believe in ghosts. And I definitely don't believe in demon voices. Those things are all explainable in some very rational, scientific manner. The problem is, there is absolutely nothing in my car that would do that, so my mind starts warping the occurrence into something bigger, something scarier, and something much, much more sinister.

What if it actually is the Devil? Am I even ready for this kind of conversation, or negotiation, rather, if I'm as up on Conversations-with-Fallen-Angels as I think I am? As much as I would love a shiny new fiddle or my own law firm, I really don't think I am prepared. Maybe I don't actually want to be in the position to make a decision if Mr. Scratch really is here to tempt me with a contract. I'm no Faust.

I screech to a stop in the neighborhood I am driving through. I turn my phone off entirely. I roll the windows up and then I turn the car off and I just sit. "Say it again. I dare you," I mutter. "I'm not afraid of you."

Nothing. "Do it!" I yell.

More nothing.

"Come on!"

Somewhere outside the car a bird chirps, breaking the stillness. I jump.

I realize that my hands are on the steering wheel for no reason whatsoever. My knuckles are turning white as I squeeze it and wait for a response. The silence begins to embolden me. "I didn't think so! Why wait until I fall asleep, huh? Come get me now!" I am yelling inside an empty car. "You want to kill me in my dreams? Well, guess what? I'll never dream again! Now what, bitch? Now what?" I have clearly lost my mind.

God, I hope the neighbors aren't watching this, I think to myself. I wait another minute until I am convinced that I could only have imagined it. Then I drive away. I turn my radio back up, and let the familiar sounds of *Appetite for Destruction* snap me back to the real world. Slash aside though, my fingers continue to drum nervously on the wheel. I just need some sleep, I lie to myself.

A few days later I find myself in my brother's driveway again, keys in hand, about to get in my car and leave. As I unlock the door he says, "I don't know if I ever told you this or not, but I figured out where those voices were coming from in my car." I have totally forgotten. How someone can totally forget a confrontation with the Devil is beyond me, yet I have.

"Yeah," he continues, "It was Moto Moto." He says it in a way that exhibits complete confidence that I will understand. I do not.

"Huh?" It seems like the right thing to say.

"Oh, sorry," he says. "I guess that didn't make any sense. He's a hippo."

"Gotcha," I say, followed by a very awkward pause. "I'm sorry, a hippo?"

He explains that his daughter had left a toy in his backseat, a talking hippopotamus from the movie *Madagascar* that operates on a motion sensor. It came in a kid's meal from a fast food place and had rolled, unknown to him, under his passenger seat. Not only does it speak, but it does so in a very deep, scary voice that says things like, "I'm every hippo's dream."

Son of a bitch.

He laughs as he tells me this, and then he reaches in the backseat of my car. He put the toy there hoping it would elicit the same creeped-out reaction from me that it did from him. "Obviously it didn't work," he chuckles disappointedly, "or you would have said something by now. Maybe the battery's dead."

"Yeah. Must be the battery," I mutter back. "That would have been funny though if it had gone off." Then without another word I get in my car and drive away.

BIGFOOT TRACKS

So maybe it's not that I don't want to believe, it's just that I've been given no real reason to. The idea of Bigfoot captures my imagination for the same reasons it captivates everyone else — the thought of something so huge and undiscovered existing in our very backyards is haunting and magical. Not some previously unknown species of shrew or frog or endangered woodpecker that no one really cares about, but a massive, hairy, man-like beast, something that looks even slightly like we do, wandering through the woods behind our houses while we sleep.

If the thought of that doesn't make your mind swim, you're broken.

That entire mysterious world begs me to explore it, though it usually ends with me watching yet another Discovery Channel documentary that reaches no conclusion whatsoever. After an hour of snippets from the Patterson-Gimlin film, a hair sample comes back inconclusive and a narrator (usually a former captain from one *Star Trek* series or another) explains that the mystery will just have to remain unsolved a while longer.

These alleged crypto-primates are everywhere. It's not just the Pacific Northwest. There are stories of similar creatures in Asia, Australia, Florida, Canada, Sumatra, and an entire host of other locations around the globe. And then there are legends of a Texas Bigfoot.

I have the opportunity to go exploring with a man that led one of National Geographic's searches for the creature. He came to one of my shows with a mutual friend, and because all my conversations turn weird at some point, the talk turned to make-believe animals. My cynicism was just enough for him to invite me out on an expedition.

While I am skeptical that the beast exists, I still do believe in being cautious, particularly when I am wandering into the wild looking for a monster. What if I'm wrong? What if it is out there? I'm brave, but I also don't want the next day's newscast to lead off with "Comedian raped by giant monkey! But first, Sports with Jim."

So into the unknown we go. Regardless of your trip leader's experience and credentials, the forest is always eerie and unnerving at one o'clock in the morning. Autumn's chilly breath is bracing, but also still and silent, disturbed only by our own soft footfalls on the pine needle carpet beneath our feet. Night-vision and thermal-imaging cameras do nothing to ease my mind, as a wall of darkness remains when I lower the goggles. It is like a horror movie, with slivers of moonlight falling through the fog and illuminating just enough of the wilderness to make me think I might just see something.

I want to bring a black guy or a hot blonde girl out on this expedition with us. They're always the first to die in those situations, and while I'm not a completely selfish person, I also won't turn down a good head start if things get bad. Hollywood has recently been making the hot Jennifer Lawrence-type the heroine however, and I would hate to go first just so that the film played well in the 18–34 year old demographic.

The strangest part of it all is the sensation of being watched out here. In a forest that should be full of animals, there is nothing. Not a deer, not a squirrel, not a raccoon. Just complete silence. Silence, and a nagging feeling that something is out there regardless of how little noise it is making. Maybe we are being watched. Maybe Bigfoot mothers take their baby Bigfeet out here to observe us for entertainment and buy little Bigfoot balloons and admission tickets for five or six pinecones apiece. A Bigfoot day at the zoo.

We find a spot to set up and then huddle in the cold October air for several hours, deciphering images in the green glow of the night vision, waiting for a sign that there is anything else alive out here among the black trees. Eventually something does begin to move, 100 yards away plodding footsteps fall somewhere out in the darkness. Within minutes, another body begins to maneuver through the trees, this time behind us, but moving in tandem with the first. These two creatures, whatever they are, move loudly, orbiting around us in an arc, mirroring the other's movements. For 15 minutes they circle us.

And then they stop as quickly as they started.

It grows quiet again, and it remains that way for another half hour. The adrenaline fades and we settle back into the silence. Then, suddenly, from only 15–20 feet away, there is an enormous crash of brush. Limbs crack and leaves shake as my guide draws his rifle and shoots to his feet. "Move! Now!" he yells. "Go! Go! Go!"

And I do. Flashlights bouncing, we scramble to the edge of the river and hurriedly follow it back to a clearing to regroup. "They do that," he says once we catch our breath. "They can get that close without making a sound." Do they really? I wonder. Is that in the textbook? How the hell does he *know* that?

So was it a Bigfoot? I have no idea. It was something large and loud that either snuck up on us quietly or that had been patiently sitting in that spot motionless for the three hours we had been out there. I know that it would be incredibly easy to leap to conclusions though. The mysterious is easy to believe in if you want to believe, and sometimes it forces its way forward even when it's the least logical explanation. Ultimately, we see what we want to see.

I watched my entire neighborhood lose its collective mind one night. I was awakened one morning at five o'clock by the sounds of people violently knocking and ringing my doorbell. This was during the string of car burglaries, so I was still sleeping on high alert. Certainly this was a neighbor warning me that the thieves were back. I rolled from bed quickly, throwing on a t-shirt and tennis shoes and flinging open the door.

The truth was much worse than I expected.

Every one of my neighbors was outside in the parking lot staring skyward at "the UFOs." Even blurry-eyed and barely awake, it was evident that what they were seeing were simply low, fast moving clouds rushing past the stars behind them, giving the appearance of motion to the otherwise stationary lights. It was an optical illusion the way a car next to you at a light might pull forward slightly, making you feel like you're rolling backwards.

But to them it was an invasion, and the presence of so many people made it impossible to argue. The mob had decided what it was seeing, and was fueling its own madness. I tried to reason with them, hopelessly. "So if the stars are spaceships, where are all the actual stars?" No answer came as they gazed into the heavens, hypnotized. "What about the Big Dipper? It's right there! Look at it!" Again, silence. Apparently constellations were just aliens flying in formation. The Interplanetary Blue Angels, if you will.

And with logic proven useless, I found myself standing in the middle of this meteorologically-induced mass hysteria, confounded and unable to stop it. If these were real aliens, I told myself, they would have already killed these dumb motherfuckers with a big bolt of blue light like in *Independence Day*. These people weren't worthy of saving. I found out the next day that the neighbor responsible for waking everyone up and convincing them that there were UFOs had been doing acid that night. Huge surprise.

You have to consider the source of a sighting, especially when the first person to point it out is tripping their balls off. Those people wanted to see aliens and they did. I would love to think that I was just 15 feet away from an undiscovered man-ape, but I doubt I was.

It's striking to me that despite all of the supposed evidence —the footprints, the grainy photographs, the voice recordings — nobody ever catches one. Not alive, and not even in focus on film. They're exactly the same as the UFOs. Perhaps they *are* UFOs. Maybe that's what the aliens look like. Perhaps the spaceship lands, Bigfoot gets out, traipses through the mud, rubs his back up against a tree, waits for a car to get close so that he can cross the street, anally probes a redneck, and then beams back up. Maybe that's why they never find a body.

Maybe all of our unanswered questions can be solved with the same creature. We can blame everything we can't explain on Bigfoot. Aliens, chupacabras, Loch Ness, the success of all these YouTube stars.

If I can't explain it, it's Sasquatch.

AN ESCAPE PLAN

Sand and water splash up behind me in a muddy rainbow. One foot flops around helplessly, as if asleep, searching for the stirrup that slipped away when this horse took off at a gallop. Brittany laughs and snaps pictures from across the beach as I cling to the animal's neck for dear life. We are somewhere in Mexico and I am making another poor decision.

My brother is getting married in the Mayan Riviera and I am perfectly content to spend this week playing on a sun-drenched beach. My class reunion is happening this same week back in my hometown, and the thought of being 1,000 miles away from my graduating class with a Modelo in my hand, while everyone I graduated with puts on little name tags, huddles up nervously in a hotel ballroom, and pretends to remember a bunch of stuff they didn't really enjoy even back then is as perfect a way to spend this week as I can imagine.

It is still a day before Jeremy's wedding and I desperately need a break from family. The allure of Caribbean water and white sand has been enough to attract the entire extended family, so both of my parents, my brother's future in-laws, my stepmom's whole side of the family, and a slew of my brother's friends are all here for the occasion. The hotel pool is the size of some small lakes and it still isn't big enough.

Two days in, and things are already claustrophobic. My parents can't stand to be in the same room as each other, or more specifically my mom and my stepmom. If the rehearsal dinner were a dagger-throwing contest instead of an actual dinner, then my mom could win first through third place using only her eyes.

To this day my mother carries herself unbelievably well around people she hates. Sure, she sometimes says things just loud enough for the other party to overhear, yet still quietly enough to not cause a disruption, but it is her body language that speaks volumes without making a scene. Her eyes are more than capable of whispering, "Bitch," and this week they are screaming.

"If she looks at me one more time —" my mom starts to say as I slip off as fast as I can to track down a quieter place to hang out for the night.

Somewhere across the resort on this very same night, my cousin Marshall will break the best man's nose, and my brothers are undoubtedly finding similar trouble. And then there is Brittany.

A free trip to Puerto Vallarta and an open bar tab still aren't enough to keep her from fighting with me. Too many different personalities are in one place, and it's a lot to handle.

"Limbo!" somebody yells, and a little Aztec runs by me with a stick. Several tourists follow him to the pool as I duck back unnoticed to my room in a desperate search for some peace and quiet.

It's how I end up here on the beach, the next day, far away from that myriad of faces. Had it been up to me, I would be here alone. Instead Brittany tags along, committed to making sure that I in no way get any time by myself on this trip. She and I rent horses from a Mexican tour guide named Juan or Jose or Miguel and ride with a group of other tourists through two miles of lush tropical forest and down to the water's edge.

It has actually been a peaceful first half of the trek to this point, our horses ambling lazily underneath the shade of the palm trees. I am riding Patrocinio, or just Patro, an amiable-enough animal that keeps stopping to nibble clumps of grass while the group moves forward ahead of us. It seems he is as tired of his companions as I am of mine, and even if I wanted to, I don't know enough about horses to convince him to move any faster.

"Hokay," Miguel says once we reach the open sand. "We are stopping for a minute if you want to take a break. But some of you, if you want to go fast, come with me, hokay?"

Of course I do. Enough with the casual Sunday afternoon stroll; I need my heart to pump. I don't listen to anything else he says, which, as I neglect to hear, happens to include that only professional riders should try this. In my mind, I am already half-way down the beach.

I lead what I think is certainly our entire group of 20 down to the water, but when I stop it is just me and one other rider, a woman in her early 30s: a professional barrel racer. She and her horse have already bonded symbiotically. Her mare moves in perfect sync with her thoughts, while Patro, now free from the confines of the forest path, jerks restlessly beneath me, sensing the open sand. "And how long have you been riding, señor?" Miguel asks me.

"Actually, I've never been on a horse before," I tell him. "But I'll be fine."

He laughs, or rather chuckles villainously, directly at me. "You are probably going to die then."

And with that, he screams something in Spanish, smacks the horse on the ass, and we shoot forward like a crash-test car, and I am every bit the dummy.

They say that time slows down when your life is in danger, that you are acutely aware of the intricacies of every moment when you are in a life threatening situation. "They" (whoever they are) are full of shit. It accelerates. Everything does — the horse, the ground scrolling beneath me, time. Everything.

Patro is not incredibly muscular; after all, he is a rental in a Mexican beach town. The regulations are, let's say, beyond lax here. Patro is probably overworked and underfed, like the Olsen twins in their teen years. I'm not certain if this is an escape plan and he thinks freedom from his captors is somewhere ahead of us over the next dune, or if dragging riders dangling from a leather strap is a hobby of his. I have been really nice to him though, I think to myself. Surely that means something. He throws his head forward and I slide a little bit more in my saddle. Now the horse is well past a lope and is in a full-blown, out-of-control sprint down the coastline towards Belize.

This isn't actually my first time on a horse, I remember. I lied to Miguel. I once spent a week at a camp with my entire fifth grade class. 200 of us set off on a massive field trip to learn the ways of the wilderness and to participate in team-building exercises while exploring our environment.

All I remember from the excursion was that my group's leader was a hippie name Randy or Rupee or Raffi, or maybe he was a Miguel too. It doesn't matter. What matters was that we rode horses that week as children. Or maybe they were donkeys. If I'd gone to my class reunion instead of coming to Mexico, I could be discussing that week at camp with some of my former classmates instead of bouncing closer and closer to a Superman-style exit off of a 40 mile per hour pony.

No, I decide, I would much rather die with shattered ribs, gurgling clear blue salt water bubbles at the ocean's edge. To me this is a better option than putting on a suit and playing High School Hierarchy with people I have intentionally fallen out of touch with. I would much rather be here. Somehow, I think Patro gets that. Instead of pitching and rolling, we level out. His uncontrolled, mad dash for freedom becomes a quick but measured gallop, as if he realizes that we are both fleeing together. My foot finds its way back in to the flapping stirrup and I unclench my hands from his mane, finding the reins. We race another half mile down the seaside before slowing to a trot.

Miguel canters up to us as we ride back, with Brittany following close behind him. My mount shakes out his mane and blows a spray of foamy saliva out of his nose, then he turns his head and gazes back down the beach while I pat his neck. Patro and I are completely on the same page. "Belize can't be that far," I whisper to him.

HARD EIGHT

I've been hiding in my hotel room as much as possible, safely distant from the blinking lights and the clanging bells of the casino floor beneath me. I walked to the showroom earlier to see the layout, and then out to the pool to avoid the mile-wide marketing ploys of my temporary employers, but now I have to go back down there. I have a show tonight at one of the Choctaw Nation's properties in Oklahoma. The flashing neon flytrap I have to walk through to get to that show causes mixed emotions.

Despite my penchant for otherwise risky behavior, I am not a big gambler. Blackjack amuses me because it offers the most control, but it's poker that tempts me. Even then, I prefer to stay out of the casino poker rooms; I would much rather shuffle my chips amongst a group of friends. The casino experience as a whole is obviously orchestrated bullshit. My job tonight is to make no bets at all. Tell jokes, collect a check, soak in the hot tub, and go home.

It's hard though.

Maddening patterns on the carpet floors keep your head up and moving. Just when you focus on one thing, another thing blinks or pops out of the corner of your eye. Look at this! No this! No that!

Ancient, wrinkled women and men lie propped up, possibly deceased, against rows of slot machines. The bars spin and stop, another loser. And another. Occasionally a distant bell signals a big winner, prolonging the myth of victory and encouraging the living dead to feed that one last $20 into the slot. Somewhere a grandchild goes without college.

A man and woman pass me in the hallway. He is furious. She is staring blankly ahead. There aren't enough lights in the world to distract her now, and even if they could, she has just cleaned out their entire bank account. I know this because the man just said, "You realize that you cleaned out our entire goddamned bank account?" This poor guy.

He must be new at this. He obviously hasn't gone through it enough times yet to keep a separate, hidden account. She still has access to his money. You're dating an obsessive gambler, I want to tell him. You can't share finances with her. You have to hide your cash like Anne Frank at Oktoberfest, you dummy. Believe me. I know. God, have I been there.

Brittany was the queen of the casino. The city I grew up in, Beaumont, is in Southeast Texas, 30 minutes west of the Louisiana border. Louisiana law makes it easy to gamble. As long as a casino isn't actually on land, the government allows it. Scattered throughout the state are riverboats, perched inches away from shore, welcoming anyone that wants to lose a few dollars inside.

Table games are forced into the waterways, but video poker is allowed everywhere. There's not a gas station or restaurant in the state that doesn't have a series of eight-liners against one wall or another. Brittany found them all. She bet just to bet. It was a compulsion. She had VIP player's cards at every one of the major casinos and the pit bosses all knew her by name.

I went with her for a while in the beginning. I quit going the first time she bit me. She had run out of money and thought she could surely win back the $600 she had just lost, if I would only give her $20. When I refused, she leaned in and bit me violently, then pickpocketed me while I inspected the wound. She went on her own after that.

She walked past security like the cast of *Ocean's Eleven*. I don't remember if that ever happened in the movie or not, but I imagine it did, and I encourage you to imagine it as well so that my comparison will make sense. Guards waved at her when she sauntered by, and you could actually see wind blow through her hair in slow motion, even indoors. Music played. Employees and regulars both greeted her by name. She strode past the patrons at the $5 and $10 dollar tables. The common folk. The riffraff. Back to the high roller room she went, the casino staff practically carrying her on their shoulders. She wasn't there to lose small amounts, dammit. She was there to lose it all.

And this wasn't a girl with a trust fund to squander, or someone with the salary of a lawyer and the accompanying pricey vice. Brittany was a waitress. She took a week's worth of tips and spun it into gold — before spinning it right back into nothing again. It's the gambler's dilemma, not knowing when to fold 'em. Brittany was good. Very good, in fact. She just wasn't good at, "Quit while you're ahead."

I remember my cell phone ringing one morning at 8:00 AM. She had been gone for two days and was finally calling.

"I'm coming home," she said. "And you're not going to believe this."

She pulled up to the apartment in a shiny, new, black Chrysler Sebring.

"What happened to the Escort?" I asked.

"I left it at the dealership when I bought this one."

"You bought a car? At 8:00 AM?"

"Yep. Told the guy I'd give him $100 if he'd unlock the door and sell it to me."

"So you won then?"

"$35,000. Blackjack. It took a while. I'm going to bed. 'Night."

"Goodnight? It's morning," I started to say, but she was already inside.

No wonder they loved her there. She partied with reckless abandon, flinging $100 chips around like quarters and almost certainly out-drinking and out-cussing everyone else at the table. When she was on, she was on. She never played it safe. Blackjack, three-card poker, craps, it didn't matter. Pass line? No thanks. Put it all on hard eight.

She fell asleep for a few hours, and then was back on the road to Louisiana immediately. She shouldn't have gone. She should have quit. Forever. She had 35,000 reasons to stop, and yet 24 hours after her nap, she had not only lost every dollar from the day before, but also an additional $20,000 that the casino had given her as a marker.

She threw the money away like a crackhead mother tossing out an unwanted baby. It couldn't have been gone faster if she'd put it directly into a dumpster. I don't know how exactly you go about losing $55,000 at a casino, but I bet it involves using the word 'fuck' a lot.

Casinos put signs up displaying a phone number to call if you have a gambling problem, but no one ever calls them. That feeling of victory. Doubling down and getting your ten. Splitting aces and watching them both hit. Seeing the dealer draw to a bust. It's an incredible endorphin rush, rivaling any drug, though she was definitely on those too.

Brittany would bet on just about anything. That was almost the only way to get her to not go gambling: bet her that she couldn't stay home.

So yes. As I pass this girl in the hallway, I recognize the look. The empty stare painted on the face of this now-penniless addict scares me a little bit. It sends a ripple of goose bumps up my arm as I walk past.

"What are we going to do about Tommy?" she asks the pissed-off guy walking ahead of her.

I don't know who Tommy is, but I'm guessing he was relying on a portion of their bank account for something important. He might be their son or her brother or a loan shark with an itchy trigger finger.

"Tommy? Fuck Tommy," says the man. "We don't even have enough gas to get home."

As the two of them make their way down the hall to the exit, I turn my gaze to follow them. Are they really going to go stand outside by the car? Maybe they're going to walk home. Maybe he will sell her into slavery for gas money. I want to be sympathetic, but that guy has to learn his lesson sometime, doesn't he?

Right now, I have my own set of problems. I have to go into a room full of shattered financial dreams and empty wallets. I have to stare at seats filled with broken souls taking advantage of a free show, probably the only thing they can still afford, and somehow figure out a way to make them laugh.

The casino wants the show clean, too. I don't work that dirty to begin with, but I still hate having the limitation thrown on my shoulders. "Our customers have high moral values," the manager tells me. "They don't use language like that." I laugh on the inside.

I can see them through the curtain from backstage. The disappointment drips silently down their faces like bitter molasses. Arms crossed, they sit in the showroom, waiting. We're out of cash, their eyes tell me. We're beaten and we're broke. Now make us laugh, Chuckle Monkey.

Yeah, I'm pretty sure that even the holiest of these people has uttered the word "fuck" once or twice in the last few hours.

I don't particularly want to walk out there right now, but I must. My opening act just said goodnight and I'm about to be introduced. The music is playing. They can't be that bad, right? This show is going to be fine, I tell myself.

And then my subconscious answers me. "Wanna bet?"

THAT DIDN'T HURT AT ALL

Fourteen-year-olds are made of different material than adults. They are the carbon fiber to my aluminum foil. I know this because I was 14 once. I started my first business then – a sprawling empire of lawns that I mowed every two weeks. It felt sprawling anyway. In reality, I only had two or three clients. Still, I had to trudge several blocks in the Texas sun to get to them, with my extension cords and trash bags and weed-eater stacked precariously on the lawnmower like a wobbly Jenga game.

I opened my first bank account with the dollars I saved and then quickly started my lifelong search for a way to make more of that money without actually doing work. I recruited another neighborhood kid to help, and soon I was making only half of the money, but doing none of the work. I was a contractor at 14. The landscaping industry was not for me, I realized. I don't like to sweat unless it's competitive. My mind does all the heavy lifting now, and until I master a way to trim grass with the Force, it's an arena I would just rather avoid. And I do.

The comedy club I've owned for the last three years is immaculate on the inside. There is a particular area around the side of the building where bushes grow, and, due mainly to my laziness, often gets out of hand. My friend Bob recently suggested that we should have a Pull-a-Weed-and-Get-In-Free night. I despise that little green patch. Therefore I ignore it.

I've decided to spend this perfect Friday afternoon clearing out that trouble spot. I'm not positive what spurred me to do it. Yard work is one of those things that, if I haven't done it in a long time, I forget that I despise it. It's like eating carrots; every now and again I try it just to reaffirm what I already know to be true.

Within 15 minutes I have broken both a lawnmower and weedeater. I spend another 20 minutes restringing a second weed-eater before deciding that I have earned a break. I sit in the shade coming up with ways to explain to the friends I've borrowed them from exactly why I have broken their equipment. I will argue briefly that the tools were faulty to begin with, before finally admitting that sometimes I'm just an idiot.

Eventually I fire up the reserve weed-eater and wade into the patch of jungle. The machine sputters and pops, its plastic wire spinning through clumps of brush and spewing cut pieces of plant life into the air like a green mist.

I consider myself to be among the lucky few on this planet in two regards: I have almost no allergies and even fewer phobias.

Poison ivy is one of the only things that I am deathly allergic to, and needles happen to be one of my few horrible fears. I had been afflicted with poison ivy only twice in my life, and both times the cure was a hypodermic syringe full of steroids. The first time, my face swelled shut. I looked like a Thanksgiving Day balloon with elephantitis. The second time I almost missed a Rolling Stones concert, but fuck that. I managed to wrap my diseased limbs in tube socks and Ace bandages like a homeless mummy and then I scratched my way through three hours of rock 'n roll.

I have no idea as I hack my way through the underbrush that I am inviting myself to experience both the poison and the puncture wounds again. As I trudge forward, little clippings of the vindictive plant flutter innocently, settling on my exposed arms, soaking in the sweat of the midday sun. Rivulets of stinging moisture run down my face. I wipe it off, inadvertently spreading it to all the places it can't get on its own. I am my own Trojan horse. Eventually I finish clearing the yard, and then pack everything into the back of a truck, sighing with the satisfaction of a job well done.

Two days later, as I sit happily pecking away at my keyboard, I catch myself scratching a rough spot on my forearm. My previous two encounters are all the prodding I need to get it looked at, except options are limited on Sundays, and it is Sunday. Still, there is a minor care center a mile away from my apartment. I can fire up my motorcycle and surely be back home within the hour.

There are 1,306 people in the waiting room when I get there, most of them sick with a cold or a headache or something else that could have been knocked out with a Tylenol. Others are way worse off. One man stands stoically in the corner waiting for a nurse to decide how to respond the report that he "almost cut his whole arm off with a hatchet." His wife is, as he so calmly puts it, "coming back with the rest of the arm any minute now." There is a little girl with a spider bite on her face, and another screaming kid that I wish a spider would bite. The chairs are all taken and the remainder of the walking wounded wander aimlessly around the room while others sprawl across the floor like unclaimed luggage.

Finally, I make it to the registration window. The receptionist is an old, black, grandmotherly-type. She hands me a form, which I complete and return a few minutes later, clearly not filled out to her satisfaction. "You left some blanks, child," she says. "I'm gonna need you to answer the rest of these questions."

"Which ones?" I ask.

"Next of kin?" she asks back.

"What? I have poison ivy. If you guys have a track record of losing patients during something as simple as giving them a shot, you need to tell me now."

"Whatever, child. Them kinda things is up to you. Just have a seat. Someone will be with you in a moment."

A "moment," I learn, is medical-speak for a period of time no less than two hours. Eventually I am escorted to a smaller room in the back for an additional hour. A series of rushed encounters follow. A a very bitchy nurse takes my blood pressure, an Indian doctor says something in Marathi or Bodo before scribbling a few runes on my chart and darting back out the door, and finally the girl comes in to actually give me the shot.

"You look nervous," she says.

"Nah, I'm good."

"It's okay. Nobody likes needles," she says. Her smile helps just a bit.

"Dislike is probably a bit of an understatement."

"If it helps," she offers, "nobody I've ever given a shot to has ever complained. They all said they didn't even know I'd done it until it was over."

This turns out to be a blatant lie. She lies the way people lie when they fill out an online dating profile. It is a flagrant fabrication designed to make her look good regardless of the truth. To begin with, the needle she brandishes looks like the tool she would choose if she was about to pierce someone's tongue or make a blanket. It is the size of one of the kindergarten pencils children use to write in Big Chief tablets. And if the needle's size isn't intimidating enough, Cortisone is not a thin liquid. It's a steroid. It is like pushing chocolate syrup and motor oil through a straw and into my right ass cheek.

"What the FUCK!?" I yell when she stabs me.

"See? That didn't hurt at all," she says with her perky little smile.

"Burn in hell," I say.

She wrinkles up her eyebrows and the smile starts to fade. "I'm sorry," she says. "I didn't mean to—"

"You lying little psycho," I fire back. I push my way past her, buckling my belt as I fight for the door. "I really need to go. Now."

"If it still hurts in the morning, you can soak it in Epsom sa—"

SLAM!

If she wasn't so cute, I'm pretty sure I might go back in and stab her to death with her own medicinal dagger. I drag my limp leg down the hall behind me, suddenly wishing for a moment that I was the guy with the simple hatchet wound. I fling the door open, causing wide eyed stares on the cattle huddled together in the lobby. "So that's why you needed my next of kin, I guess?!" I yell.

The old black woman behind the glass stares a knowing stare. She knew. She *knew* that stabby nurse was a menace. There is understanding in her eyes as she watches me hobble out. "Poor child," I can hear her say.

I fire up my bike and squeal out of the parking lot. Taking my motorcycle is the second worst decision I've made today. Every pothole hurts. Even the tiniest bump sends shards of electric glass ricocheting through my nervous system. I can't believe how poorly thought out my plan is. George W. Bush had a better exit strategy than I do.

Eventually the poison ivy subsides, but my days of landscaping are through.

Forever.

AND SOMEWHERE THERE IS LAUGHTER

If you ever want to make God laugh, tell him your plans. Woody Allen said it originally, but it's my dad's voice I hear when the phrase echoes in my head. It is December, five days before Christmas. My father is going in for heart surgery in the morning and I am headed to our nation's capital to tape a special for satellite radio. I call him from the balcony of my Los Angeles apartment. I shiver in the cold and smoke a cigarette as we talk.

"I have the flights all booked," I say proudly. "I go to DC for the weekend and then I'll be in Texas on Sunday in plenty of time for Christmas." My itinerary is perfect. "No," I tell him. "I can't stay for the New Year. I'm headed to Oakland and then driving back to Los Angeles from there. I have it all figured out."

"If you ever want to make God laugh," he says.

"Yeah, yeah," I say, chuckling. "Everything's going to be fine. I'll call you when I get to DC and see how the surgery went."

"I love you, son," he says.

"I know."

My father and I had our ups and downs through most of my life. Some of my earliest memories are the sounds of my parents fighting loudly as I try to sleep. I'm just shy of nine years old when they divorce, and I am sitting in my dad's little blue truck when he tells me. The black plastic, fake-leather seats are cracked and smell like cigarette smoke. The engine idles as we sit in the parking lot that evening after soccer practice. I am too young to know what he means when he says that he isn't going to be living with us anymore.

I go from eight to 30 quickly, and our relationship swings back and forth dramatically throughout those 22 years. Some memories are stronger than others but most are just flashes of moments, captured in fuzzy still-life like Polaroids.

I'm nine. I'm walking the top row of the bleachers like a high-wire artist. My dad is at the bottom talking to the woman who will eventually become my stepmom. I'm eleven. Willie Nelson and Ray Charles sing *Seven Spanish Angels* in the living room as my dad adjusts the knobs on his new stereo and I lay on the floor. I'm 13. I tell him that I'm not going with him when he comes to pick me and my brothers up for the weekend. "I hate your stupid church," is the excuse I give before I run back inside.

There are pictures in my mind with no dates on them. I could be 12 or 20. He has dogs, one after the other, most of them puffy little balls of white. Fritchie. Beignet. Max. There is a kitchen table with a bench on one side. I ripped my finger open on the lid from a can of Pringles at that table. You can still see the scar. The ceiling of the game room upstairs is covered in the models I build, painstakingly painting them and straightening the decals. Airplanes of every sort hang like icicles over the pool table.

When I am 21, my grandmother, his mother, goes into the hospital. My dad paces the halls there waiting for the inevitable bad news from the doctors. I can't imagine how he is strong enough to face the death of a parent.

I land in DC and make my way to the hotel. My phone rings as I unlock the door to my room. "Dad's in a coma," my brother tells me. "He never came around after surgery."

"I have a flight in the morning," I tell him, then hang up the phone in silence. I slide down the wall onto the floor of the hallway, staring blankly in front of me. I have a show in two hours.

The club is packed with people when I walk in and I hate every single one of them. I have spent my entire life mocking the general population, with their real jobs and their fluorescent lighting and their boring offices. Tonight I want desperately to hide in a cubicle, to type the time away at some keyboard with no one staring at me. This is the tradeoff, I realize. Now, not only do I have to pretend to be happy myself, I have to make other people happy on top of it.

My grandmother on my mom's side, long before I ever started doing comedy, used to say how amazing it was that Jack Benny was able to perform while his son was dying. I understand it now.

I stay on stage for one and a half hours, somehow removed from, while still aware of, my sadness and fear. The stage will always remain the one place where I still feel completely in my element, regardless of what is going on around me. Jack Benny must have gotten that.

I walk off the stage and back into the dark reality that is now my life. I cancel my next few months' of shows before I even get on the plane the next day. I am going to stay in Houston indefinitely.

It is Christmas Eve, three days later. I send my brother home to spend the evening with his wife and daughter. I am stationed in the lobby between visitation periods, aimlessly flipping through a book, waiting for the next opportunity to stare down at my father and hope for a response. I walk into the cafeteria late, hoping for something to eat.

"How are you today?" the lady behind the counter asks.

My question is a simple one, and the words fall out of my exhausted lips like leaves from a dying tree. "How late are you open?"

She repeats herself. "HOW are YOU today?"

"How LATE are you open?" I try again.

"I asked how you were today."

"I am in the hospital on Christmas Eve," I say, bouncing my tray loudly on the metal rails. "How late ... are you ... fucking open?"

"Sir, you don't have to use—"

"Maybe you should just slosh some mashed potatoes on the plate next to my chicken fried steak, pick up your minimum-wage-based check, and take your soulless body away from people that really don't care how fucking chipper you pretend to be around the holidays."

I wish I'd said that.

Instead I simply leave my tray on the line and wander off. I don't think I want to be here alone.

Days roll by, and I spend every one in that very same lobby. It is a waiting game. Just wait. There are no other options. You can wait, or you can wait. For 20 minutes at a time, five times a day, seven days a week, and then all the time in between. There is nothing you can do to change the situation. Friends call. "I'm sorry," they say, but they don't know. Or maybe they do, but they're not in this lobby like I am at the moment. Or the next moment. Or the thousands of moments still to come.

My youngest brother, Hunter, is still in Hawaii. He moved there on a whim with one bag and nowhere to stay. He just got off a plane in Honolulu two months ago and carved out a niche for himself there somehow. He wants to come back now to be involved but he doesn't have a plan. My car is still at my apartment in Los Angeles, and the goal becomes to find a way to get him there so he can drive it back for me.

Coordinating a trip for Hunter has always been like playing Plinko. No matter how much planning you try to do, that little plastic disc is just going to end up wherever the hell it wants to go.

We sort out his flight and I arrange to have him picked up at LAX. I have everything arranged actually — a place to stay, my car keys, and enough cash to get him back to Texas. All he has to do is get on the plane. Whether he gets distracted by a shiny object or simply gets lost, I don't know, but he misses his flight. To his credit he does try to come up with an alternative plan. "I can catch a flight into San Francisco instead," he says.

"Of course," I tell him. "Go right ahead. It's only seven hours from L.A. Great job, Magellan." Eventually he does make it back, though I will never manage to find out exactly how. I am actually worried more about my vehicle than I am about him. Not that I don't love him, but I have two other brothers; that is my only car.

Days turn into weeks, and the diagnosis grows more and more grim. There have been a series of strokes and his brain activity is virtually nonexistent. On January 17th, the decision is made. The family gathers in the small, now private room. Goodbyes are said, tears are shed, and the breathing machine is removed. He is gone. The tension hangs like humidity in the air, thick and suffocating. My brother Jeremy and I turn to each other and embrace, heads buried in each other's shoulders.

I feel something move as we stand there — a vibration — down my upper leg. It is awkward as we hold each other.

"Tell me that was your phone," he says.

"God, I hope so," I reply, and in the most unlikely of places, we laugh hysterically.

It's been ten years now and some things have faded. Sometimes I get disappointed in myself when I realize that I've let more than a day or two pass without thinking of him. How could I forget? Then, out of the blue, a day or so later, I'll pick up the phone to call him. I'll stop myself as I scroll down to the D's. "Damn. He really would have gotten a kick out of that story," I tell myself.

Or maybe he will flash into my head over a bowl of Cookies & Cream ice cream covered in chocolate syrup. I use to eat it at his house on Saturday nights after everyone had gone to bed. Just me, sitting on his living room floor watching television.

The comfort is there now though. I don't have to carry it every day. The memory has disappeared and resurfaced enough times that I know it will never go away for good. It seems like an eternity since I stood on that balcony with my big plans for the future. I was going to take over the world, and he was going to have his heart fixed. I've readjusted my plans now though, to compensate.

And somewhere, I'm sure, there is laughter.

THROUGH A FROZEN SEA

The Gulf Coast of the United States is a self-contained biosphere. The selection of things you can do to entertain yourself is as unique as the culture, and boats piloted by crusty Cajun sea captains are as abundant as the restaurants selling étouffée and crawfish. Frequently, chartered trips leave the Louisiana shores on expeditions out into deep water where adventurers hunt for yellowfin tuna hiding beneath the waves.

It is a few weeks after my father's death, and I am leaving on one such voyage out of Venice, Louisiana. Virtually unknown until the 2010 BP oil spill, Venice is a bit removed from the regular, beaten path. If you're unfamiliar with its exact location, it is seven hours east of Houston and two hours south of New Orleans. From there, you drive to the end of the world, go through a frozen sea, past the dead floating bodies of pirates that have lost their way, and over a giant waterfall.

Venice is eleven miles past that.

My grandfather was an avid fisherman his entire life and instilled a love of the sport in me. From the day I could walk, I can remember standing on jetty rocks and throwing my line into the deep. A cooler full of redfish and speckled trout would accompany me and my grandfather home, where my grandmother would fry them up along with a crisp batch of sweet potato fries. My childhood is a collection of Saturday afternoons filled with the smell of hot oil in the air and a pan full of freshly cooked, corn-meal-covered fish on the table.

I cannot begin to count the nights that I've spent on one beach or another, stoking a fire to burn away the dark's chill and waiting for the first fingers of sun to reach over the horizon. Mornings spent waist-deep in the ocean with a fishing rod in my hand have always been the most peaceful, even if not necessarily safe. When you're in the water, it is seldom efficient to walk back to shore with every fish caught. A stringer tied to a belt loop will often suffice, with each fish added to the string until you hit your limit. I vividly recall having had that string hit by a massive force and jerked out towards deeper water before the pressure released. Pulling it in, the half of a fish dangling off the end is all that is needed to remind you that sharks are quite present. They're usually blacktips though, and I have shared the water with them my entire life.

I scuba dive around them all the time now, but they are childhood companions of mine. As teenagers, we used to fish specifically for them, swimming out to the second or third sand bar with a fishing pole and a piece of bloody meat attached to a large hook, casting from the shallower water, and then swimming back with the pole to wait for an indication of a hit. Swimming with blood-drenched chunks of flesh through the murky gulf probably doesn't rank high on the Brilliant-Things-I've-Done-In-My-Life list, but it is exhilarating.

And though I've spent a lot of my life on the water, I have never been offshore to fish. I only know the tales of snapper and tuna that my friends bring back with them when they go out. This trip will change that.

Jeremy calls me to meet him at the last minute. We need a break after the funeral, he says. He and his friend Scott have chartered a boat and the other two people going with them had to back out suddenly. Our cousin Marshall and I have been called in as replacements. I am the only rookie on the tour. Offshore fishing is a regular pastime for Jeremy. Scott is a lawyer who owns his own boat and goes out frequently on the Gulf down in South Texas. Marshall has worked as a hand on one vessel or another for most of his life. It is the perfect crew, so long as I can manage to hold myself together and not screw things up.

"You're gonna get sick," Marshall tells me. "It's okay though. Everyone does their first few times. Just make sure you throw up over the side."

"And you may want to take it easy on the alcohol tonight," my brother adds. We are sitting on the deck of the house boat at the fish camp and I have just poured another massive glass of Jack Daniels, sans mixer. I've always found it disrespectful to the whiskey gods to add anything but ice, and even that is situational. The three of them have been there for a day already and are well rested. On the other hand I have just driven seven hours from Texas.

"I'll be fine," I say confidently. Everybody chuckles together at my ignorance, and then Scott begins to brief me on what to expect aside from the inevitable sea sickness. The weather's been bad he says, but a hole is opening up in the morning, and that's when we are going. It is January, so it is going to be cold, but worth it. On top of it all, he's found the perfect captain and the perfect boat. Money can't buy a better trip, he swears jubilantly. And then he is interrupted by the skipper himself.

Although Scott is a bloodthirsty demon of a fisherman, he has gone to great lengths to find a captain who is even sicker than he is. Captain Al is the kind of guy that goes spearfishing for mako sharks in his down time. Just him, a pointy stick, and 500 lbs of muscle and teeth in the water at the same time. I have always considered myself somewhat brave for diving with my handful of blacktips, but this man chooses to virtually French kiss the fastest fish in the ocean for fun. He is a young version of Captain Quint.

"I don't want anyone in this goddamn boat that doesn't want to kill stuff!" he begins. "You got that? This isn't a goddamn pleasure cruise! We're coming back with fish, and if we can't catch 'em and reel 'em in, then I'll stick raw meat in my pockets, jump in, and bite them to death myself. I'm serious here, people. We're going to war! Do you hear me?! WAR!

I know where they are. If they're not there, I know where they're hiding. We will hunt these fish down, and we will kill them. We will kill their families. We will kill every one of their goddamn fish friends. We'll even kill other fish that might owe them money. Nothing is safe out there! I swear to God, if I have to put hooks in my face and swim down there and wake 'em up, we're coming back with fish. Now get some goddamn sleep, girls! We leave at 6:00 AM."

With that, he slams a double shot of Jack and goes to bed.

Following his lead, the four of us retire as well. Final advice is given to me as we drift off in our bunk beds. Scott's multiple off-shore trips a month qualify him to brag. With the starched, white button-ups and the propriety of the courtroom left back at home, the real Scott comes out to explain his strategy for soaking up the sure-to-come excitement of the next day.

"No cameras. That's the first rule," he says in a heavy drawl. "There are a lot of things that not everybody gets to experience and this here's one of 'em. I don't carry a regular camera and I don't carry a video camera and I don't carry any of them other kinds of cameras. Y'all gettin' what I'm sayin' here?" He is drunk, and his Texas accent gets thicker with every word.

"I don't neeeeeeed a camera 'cause I keep all the pictures right here in my head. Right here." It is pitch black here in the bunk room, but I assume he is pointing at his head. He continues. "You can't print it, because it's all in my brain. There's a lot of stuff up there that no one will ever get to see. Places I've been. Fish I've caught. Memories that will never go away."

There is a long pause.

"A lot of fat girls in there, too," he finishes.

We fade off into sleep with perfectly justified high expectations for the next day, and then somewhere as we slumber, Murphy's Law creeps in.

We awake the next morning to find Captain Al storming up and down the dock and screaming into a cell phone. As we make our way out of the house boat he finishes his call and informs us that our plans have changed.

"Someone stole my goddamn gear in the middle of the night! I don't know who it was yet, but when I find that sick sonofabitch, I'm gonna cut him the fuck up, eat some of him, and feed what's left of his ass to the goddamn pelicans! But don't worry," he adds. "I got everything under control."

Not only has all of his equipment been stolen, but the weather is deteriorating as well. Still, Al has arranged a replacement boat and a new captain to take us out in his stead. It is up to us to decide whether we are going to attempt to salvage the trip or not, and like any group of testosterone-driven, still-slightly-drunk males, of course we do.

The four of us climb into the new boat and head 50 miles out to the Midnight Lump, a salt dome in the Gulf of Mexico that is legendary among deep sea anglers. The three of them laugh a bit more at me, satisfied that I am going to lose what little food I had eaten somewhere on the ride out, and I am not very confident myself. I have never been this far out on a boat before. I drove seven hours, slept very little, and I've eaten even less.

It is 40° outside before the spray hits, and when that happens it drops to absolute zero. The water temperature would not be an issue if it was avoidable, but the seas are raucous, as if Poseidon had gone on a drinking binge the night before as well, and was still at it. The two-to-four foot waves we were expecting quickly turn into 15 foot swells which we seem to be hitting at 140 mph. That may be a bit of writer's embellishment on my part, but still, barreling through four-to-six foot waves in a fast boat just sucks.

If you haven't done it, do this instead. Crawl into a rock tumbler, put that in a clothes dryer, get someone to push the whole thing off a mountain, land on a trampoline, and bounce into the side of a moving train.

While you have to pee.

Charter services usually provide bean bag chairs so the passengers can flop down on the ride out to deep water. They do it because the bags absorb a lot of the impact as the bottom of the boat smacks the surface between swells. That, and who doesn't love bean bags? I roll over in mine to see my brother's face buried in his rain slicker. He looks slightly green, which is weird, because I feel perfectly fine.

I pull myself up to the center console to watch the waves as we hit them. As I do so, I notice my cousin attempting to hang his head over the rail. Every time he tries to throw up, he is launched backward and away from the side. "Are you okay?" I ask.

"I will be. Gimme a bit," he replies, groaning.

"So when does it get bad?" I ask. "Because this is great so far!"

He rolls his eyes upward at me from the deck. "You. Shut. Up."

Scott is in a similar position on the other side of the boat, retching violently into an even more violent sea. The grey rain runs in ice cold rivulets down his brow as he turns to me. "How the fuck … are you … not throwing uh—" he manages to ask before his head flops forward again.

I don't have an answer for him. It is a bit disturbing to find that my body doesn't consider any of this abnormal enough to react to it. Then again, where is the difference between being out on this water and any of the other things I've forced my body through over the last two decades? Years of riding rivers, climbing rocks, jumping out of planes, combat landings, and sideways helicopters, and a million other things have probably made my body feel like it is on vacation bouncing around in these waves.

I hold onto whatever I can find, savoring every moment of the new realization that my body is at home on this rolling sea. The butterfly feeling hits my stomach and leaves again, only to return as we launch off another wave, liquid railroad tracks hit with no brakes. I let go of the rail for as long as I can, only to be tossed haphazardly back onto my beanbag. I claw my way back upright to do it again. "Woooooohoo!" I yell as the spray washes over my face.

If there is a letdown at all, it is finding out that you can't catch big fish without a boat full of people working together, and all of my more experienced companions are incapacitated. I am left to enjoy the rollercoaster ride by myself as we head back in.

"We'll have to do this again when the weather is better," my brother says as another plume of icy water breaks over us. "It's way more fun."

"I don't know how it could be," I say. "This is amazing!"

AS I WALK THROUGH THE VALLEY

It is mid-afternoon somewhere just north of Mexico. I am leaning back in my chair, feet up on an old cable spool, watching the sweat drip off my beer as I hold it against my forehead. Mesquite trees punch out of the dirt like escaping corpses to block the sun, letting just enough blue sky through to make the day perfect. Sam and I are on tour in South Texas, and today is almost good enough to make me forget yesterday.

This juxtaposition on the road is something I am familiar with. Often a horrible day is followed by a surprisingly amazing one. You never know. You can't predict it. Even when I return to places I've been before, the experience is never the same. I've walked into gigs at dive bars expecting the worst and have had some of the best shows of my life. I have also driven places thinking that nothing could possibly go wrong and somehow the world still found a way to explode in front of me like a schizophrenic landmine.

I've done this same run through the Rio Grande Valley before, and while I can never quite nail down what the crowds might be like, I can always count on at least part of the trip to work out for the best. You just never know.

Isaac owns the theater downtown that I am playing tonight. One of the greatest perks to traveling like I do is that I've made friends in every cupboard and corner of the world — happy souls in Africa and Bahrain and Saudi Arabia and Japan that I always attempt to spend time with when I am aimed in their direction. The same holds true in the States, and, even more so. I get to meet people I would never run into otherwise. Sometimes those people even work themselves into my more intimate circle of friends. Isaac is one of those people.

We're staying at his house while we're in town. No half-star hotel room for these few days — his house is inviting and comfortable, eclectic and interesting. Mexican art hangs on every wall, some his, some other artists. Crosses dot the few uncovered spaces, and skeletons and statues and sculptures sit on antique tables in every corner. The front door is carved ornately and looks 1,000 years old. In every room, the walls are one earthy-rich color or another. It is not museum-like though. Projects sit half-finished if you stop to look. A sketch in progress. A pot on the stove. Instrument cables run to amplifiers from a makeshift jam session in the living room. The bench sits pulled out at the piano. A speaker stack is set up in the corner for no apparent reason at all. The place feels happily used, like a sports car that the owner actually drives.

Isaac is many things: a musician, an artist, a chef, a nightclub owner, and a completely free spirit. The first time I met him we sat on the patio at his restaurant and ate paella and fried cilantro, and after so many trips through this area, he and I have become friends. That's why we're staying at his place this week. I need to press the reset button after the first night out here.

The Valley is basically just North Mexico. The threat of violence hovers, ominous, like a cloud at the border. I usually slip into Reynosa or Progreso for street tacos and some dollar beers while I'm down here, but not this time. I couldn't even escape the feeling of tension while on our side of the river.

After a surprise change in our itinerary, Sam and I showed up for an extra show we tagged onto our theater sets at Isaac's place. The hotel was a crime scene. Literally. It was fairly evident that someone might have been killed there in the last few days. I rarely walk barefoot in hotels; socks just seem safer. I kept my shoes on in this one.

The first key they gave me led to an already inhabited space, though the tenants were either dead or gone or both. Smoldering cigarettes in the ashtray filled the room with smoke, a hazy veil hanging in the air like an Ecuadorian forest, and on the other side of that fog could have been anything from a murdered body to an old Chinese man selling Mogwai. Scattered clothes and toiletries littered the room. The space immediately downstairs was occupied by a dog, a German shepherd from the sounds of it, which barked incessantly. Throaty woofs and growls pierced the walls as I went back to trade in my key for another room, though the new one was no cleaner than the one with the missing people in it. It's one night, I told myself. Just one night. Suck it up.

I awoke the next morning to a sound at my door. Growing up with three brothers has made me a light sleeper. Any noise is an attack. Catatonia to alertness is instant. My subconscious always seems to know when something is not right, and something was definitely not right. It wasn't a knock at the door that woke me up, but something much more subtle. I slipped off the side of the bed and stole a glance around the corner. The door was open slightly, as far as the security latch would allow anyway, and a hand was reaching through attempting to flip the latch open. I took two quick steps and kicked the door. The hand crunched and popped loudly as someone on the other side screamed in pain. I held my foot in place as the fingers twitched.

"What do you want?" I yelled, keeping my weight against the door.

"Housekeeping."

I pulled my leg back, flipped the bolt, and jerked the door open.

"Have you lost your fucking mind?" I said. The man pulled his hand in to his chest, cupping it like an injured bird. His manager strode over, a cocky looking, Napoleonic half-man with a deep Indian complexion.

He ignored his employee with the injury; a mere battlefield casualty. "Checkout was at 11:00 AM," he said. "Why are you still here?"

"Checkout is at noon," I shot back.

"No, it's not."

"It's on the sign on the back of this door, you fucking idiot. And it is 11:06 right now"

"Oh, well … that's wrong."

"So that's why you're breaking into my room?"

"We knocked and no one answered, so we assumed someone must be passed out in the room." He was smug. Call the police, his face said. I dare you.

"That was your immediate assumption? Why didn't you call?"

"Your phone must be broken."

"Like your friend's hand?" I asked, and flung the door shut. "Give me a minute," I yelled through the closed door.

Sam meets me in the lobby, only to share his own story. He was in the shower when he noticed a shadow through the shower curtain. Another employee had bypassed his safety lock in a similar fashion and caught him off guard, but left when the 250 lb black man stepped naked into the room.

Sam left to pull the car around. As I made my way around to meet him, three of the owner's friends were trying to block my exit. "What you wanna do, bitch?" one of them asked, posturing in front of the other two while the owner stood by and watched. A single tear tattooed on the man's face indicated that if things escalated this wouldn't be his first violent altercation.

"Seriously?" I asked, trying to limit myself to just that one word. There were three of them and I can be dumb sometimes when I'm angry. I walked to the car while they circled, expecting a punch to be thrown, though one never came. They got louder as I got in the car, and I popped back out of the passenger seat to yell something in reply but was jerked back in by the belt loop by Sam. No one ever believes that he is the calmer of the two of us when we're on the road. Looks are deceiving, I suppose.

So now, at Isaac's, I am better. Ceci, his girlfriend, is cooking a homemade Mexican dinner for us back at the house. From inside the bar, far across this wide open back lot, old Johnny Cash, the good stuff, plays on the jukebox and the crack of pucks on the shuffleboard table float out of the open door and off into the air. Another round of beers comes out.

I mention the hotel story to Isaac. "That kind of thing is getting worse down here." he says. "They buckled down on the gangs and cartels on the Mexico side so now they just bring it here. Happens all the time, too. That lady whose husband got killed on the jet ski on Falcon Lake? The investigator on the Mexican side got his head cut off. They're ruthless. There was a guy down here that got in trouble with one of the cartels and they kidnapped his baby and fried it. Literally. Like fried it."

"You're kidding," I say.

"No. I wish I were. It's bad bro."

"They fried it."

"I'm serious."

"They don't even do that at the fair. I mean, they'll do butter or Oreos ..."

"You're sick, bro. You know that, yes?"

I do know it, but it's how I deal with things. I made a fried baby joke. I take a sip of my beer and think about that for a second. What kind of person does that? As I mull it over, I hear Sam doing an impression of a mock Visa commercial.

"When you come to Mexico make sure you bring your Visa card, because they'll take your baby ... but they won't take American Express." I laugh harder than I should. They always talk about paying dues on the road, and while I have certainly paid my share — more than enough to not really have to deal with subpar accommodations anymore, much less gang-run hotels — when those moments do surface I have learned to take them in stride. You can't let the negativity shake you or your sense of humor. Good nights or bad, you can never stop laughing with your friends.

"That fried baby joke was fucked up, bro," Isaac says, laughing.

"It's good to see you again, too," I reply, and we clink bottles, content to wash away the Valley with cold beer and camaraderie.

STUPID ROCKS

I'm supposed to be too old for this shit. That's the Danny Glover coming out in me, even as the water rushes past in the cool shadows of the canyon. I'm working my way through the Wadi Mujib in northeastern Jordan and my body is fighting me. It's part ropes course, part hike, and it weaves its way through a gorge cut into the rock some 1,400 feet below sea level. It is smack in the heart of the lowest region on Earth. As the river rages, I wade onward. Every step is a gamble of course. Just below the surface sit rocks of various shapes and sizes, and between them, ankle-wrenching divots and crevices. This isn't America, that's for sure.

America would have rubber-cornered the whole park. We are terrified of lawsuits, and rightfully so. Every billboard reminds you that if a company makes even the slightest misstep, The Texas Hammer or the Strong Arm or the Gangster of Law is going to get them! Did you pour a bucket of hot coffee on your own face? Someone is obviously to blame. Let's get them too! The Legal Monster is on your side!

To go on an "adventure," you have to wear a helmet and knee pads. Probably elbow pads too. Just put on this bubble wrap and this bear suit and go have fun. So much equipment, in fact, that individuals would be unrecognizable to the lifeguards stationed every 20 feet, blowing whistles and chastising you against anything that resembles risk, until the entire journey is sapped of any sort of fun.

That's not the case here. Not in Jordan. I grab nothing more than a lightweight lifejacket on my way to the ladder down into the canyon, and then it's a free-for-all. A latticework of rope fills one void, a caution not to take that route. It's more of a suggestion though; I can go anywhere I want. The depth of the river varies from ankle to chin-deep. I decide I want to scale a portion of the rock wall and leap back into one of the deeper pools. My Americanized mind glances around for someone to tell me no. On cue, a park employee rounds the bend, bobbing through the rapids. I'll wait for him to pass, I think.

He slips past me in the current, catches a cleft in the rock with his hand, then scrambles up the exact line I was contemplating. His muscles are sinew and he makes it look simple. He jumps up and out, splashing dangerously close to my head as I duck out of the way. He's not here to caution anyone. His whole job is probably just to tell people to go faster and remove the occasional dead body.

I try to take the rock myself, but a lifetime of these sorts of things has taken its toll. The cartilage in my left knee is shredded. I did it in Peru in the Andes, and stand up comedians don't exactly carry the greatest insurance policies. Still, I try. I am halfway up when my foot slips, and despite distributing my weight, I grind down the slick face shin first. It shaves off a two-inch strip of hair and skin as I splash back down to the water.

I probably just need to eat, I think. That's my rationalization. If it weren't for the lack of food and water, I could have easily made it up. It is Ramadan here after all.

Should you contemplate a trip to the Middle East, I recommend avoiding the whole ordeal, this ninth month of the Islamic calendar, the Holy month of Ramadan. I'll be honest, I struggle with the Islamic faith. Stateside we only discuss it when an act of terrorism occurs. We speak of radical Muslims and the dangers of zealots who act on their religious dictums, but most people don't really have any idea what the faith entails at all.

I don't believe that Islam as it is practiced by the majority of the world is a violent religion. I don't. It is weird as hell to me though. The sheer amount of work required to practice is overwhelming. I've visited many mosques in my travels, from the Blue Mosque in Istanbul to the Sheikh Zayed Grand Mosque in Abu Dhabi. They've all been aesthetic visits however, trips to photograph the architecture and the surface culture. I finally made myself take a tour of the Grand Mosque in Bahrain to get a better idea of what exactly being a practicing Muslim involves.

That mosque looms over the Manama horizon. I couldn't count the times I'd walked past it before I made myself enter and ask questions. It turns out that Muslims pray up to five times a day. It begins with ablution, a washing of sorts. They wash their feet and face, which is simple in a mosque. There are places designed specifically for it. In Middle Eastern airports though, it gets a little weird. At prayer time you might find yourself in a bathroom suddenly full of men washing their feet in the sink. It can be shocking if you're not expecting it. It's jarring even if you are.

After the ablution, you pray. You acknowledge that Allah is the greatest. You say that a bunch of times. Then you repeat a series of verses from the Koran, the holiest book of all books ever written. You bow a lot. You sort of sing your words. There are lots of rules, and if I haven't repeated this enough, you do it five times a day. Part of the muezzin's call to the morning prayer, if you happen to live close enough to the speakers that blare from the minarets of a mosque, yells that prayer is more important than sleep.

I respect the tenacity that it takes, and I am even more respectful of the way some people need it to get through their day, but I still can't find a way to take it seriously. It doesn't gel with what I know about the world. Then again, America is full of people eating Jesus crackers and letting old men splash water on their heads. I guess dogma of any sort freaks me out.

Ramadan is the extreme embodiment of these beliefs. During that holy month, Muslims are not allowed to consume anything from dawn to dark. Not food, not water, not anything. Breathing is somehow allowed, I suppose because it is involuntary. If it weren't I'm sure there would be a rule against it too. As a Westerner visiting during this time, it is almost impossible to find any normalcy. Restaurants are closed until dusk. You are relegated to ordering room service. Most hotels will give you a page of guidelines to follow during this period. They all begin the same way:

Non-Muslims are in no way forced to follow the traditions of Ramadan.

You're not forced to participate in them the same way you're not forced to participate in abstinence if a nuclear bomb destroyed all life on earth but you. It's the part where my brain breaks down. I understand choosing to fast in an effort to strengthen your bond with others who share your faith. I do not understand being offended by seeing someone else eat who doesn't buy into your particular brand of witchcraft.

So I am starving in this canyon. I'm also frustrated and bleeding. It's not that important anyway, I tell myself. I've been here before.

There is a rock somewhere off the coast of Cape Zanpa in the East China Sea on the Okinawan coast. It's one of those cliff diving rocks. It stands all regal in the blue water, a pool of infinite depth just below it, and a path of easily-navigable-enough rock steps carve their way up to its top. I remember climbing it a decade ago so I could lie in the sun and watch the fighter jets take off from Kadena Air Base. The problem with being up there was that I realized the jump was possible. It was probably only a 30 foot drop, but from the top it looked like Felix Baumgartner's Red Bull leap from space.

I played my mind games, naturally.

"Jump," said the rock.

"Fuck off," I said back.

But the rock taunted me. It dared me. Adrenaline is my vice, and the rock knew it. After the first day of sitting at the top, I tried everything in my power to convince myself that it didn't matter. It's just a rock. Rocks are dumb and old and can't do a whole lot. Stupid rock. "You can't tempt me."

But it did. All night long. I finally went back and jumped the next day.

I'm in Jordan now though, ten years and half a globe removed from that Okinawan cliff jump. I make it to the end of the canyon. I play in the pools at the base of the waterfall. I've cracked my head twice on the rocks along the way, wondering the whole time if all our helmet laws have some merit after all. No, I decide. I like my freedom to die just fine.

It is on the way back out of Wadi Mujib, when I've almost forgotten about the unscaled wall, that I pass it again. My friend Trenton watched my attempt on the way in, and just as I am about to float out of sight, I hear him splash behind me. He made the climb when I wasn't watching, took the leap, and now I have to do it.

I push back against the current, a new drive kicking in. To hell with this rock too. My toe finds a wet hold but sticks. I spread my weight out, slip my fingers over the also-wet ledge and stretch up. I slip again, this time carving a gouge out of my other shin. I don't fall all the way though. This time my foot catches. So does my hand. Suddenly I am throwing one leg over the top. The jump is anticlimactic, but it never really was about the jump. It's about going where I couldn't.

It's much later now, and we've ducked into one of the more liberal resorts that dot the Dead Sea. I've eaten and had a few beers, and wandered into the salty water. The salinity of the Dead Sea is some eight times that of any regular body of salt water. Pain shoots through my nervous system as I walk in, my fresh scrapes burning like pepper spray in a paper cut.

I lie back, the water supporting me like a toy boat. The setting sun drifts down behind the mountains of Israel across the water, and I've never felt more alive.

WAITING FOR THE SUN

I have seen more of the Middle East than I ever expected a kid from a small town in Southeast Texas would see. I won't pretend that my time there has been completely positive, but it has been eye-opening. Iraq, Kuwait, Yemen, Qatar, Jordan, Abu Dhabi, Dubai, Bahrain, Saudi Arabia ... they all start to bleed together, a mixture of people in ghutras and thobes and burqas speaking harsh-sounding languages I have never managed to figure out. It's not a slight to the region or its people, but it is an acknowledgment that it is not the magical land of Aladdin and Scheherazade of our imaginations. The romanticized world of the Arabian Nights gets lost somewhere between the airport and your destination.

I am flying from Washington, DC this time with Sam, and we're meeting another comic named Katsy in Kuwait. Katsy is an upbeat, sassy black woman from Los Angeles. Katsy has no "off" switch, and I quickly realize that the pressure is definitely not going to be on me to have to entertain anyone off stage. Her mouth is a machine of energy and stamina, her thoughts are projectiles launched at anyone that passes. Questions, answers, ideas, laughter — when she eats, her food has to turn sideways and tiptoe to get in around the words.

I don't know exactly how old she is, but it's become the subject of discussion over the last few days. Comedians tend to latch on to one thing and drive it into the ground. We will take a subject and exhaust every possible angle on it, and then laugh even harder at how frustrated people get when we won't leave it alone, and with Katsy, that thing is her age.

Initially she can't remember our names, changing our identities from Sam and Slade to Quincy and Slam Bam. Then one of us fires off an Alzheimer's joke and we all know it's just a matter of time before this spirals out of control.

"You can talk about my age if you want," she says, "but it just means that I've seen things you haven't."

"Yeah. Like the 1800s," I say, rolling around in the back seat with laughter.

A day later the three of us, along with our security escorts and a Sergeant named White, climb on board a boat — a heavily armed 30 foot Army SeaArk — and head out into the Persian Gulf. Once we clear the harbor and get out into open water, the captain turns around toward us. "You want to drive?" he asks.

"I'm going first!" Katsy yells, and sprints to the driver's seat.

"You better hold on," Sergeant White says, and we do.

Katsy hits the throttle and the bow of the boat shoots ahead. Not content with simply going fast and straight, she hits a comfortable speed and then throws the boat into a hard turn, almost tossing our Marine escort in the Gulf. She pulls down on the lever and then hammers it forward again, cutting through the rolling wake left by the bow as it slides sideways through the water. Waves rush onto the open deck in the back where we hold on to the rails and roof and attempt to stay on board.

She spins the boat into another donut and then circles back through it again. The cameraman falls down. More water gushes on board, soaking us below the waist. Her yells echo over the sound of the engine as White comes crashing into me. We hang on.

"When is it my turn?" Sam tries to ask.

"Wooooooohoooooo!" screams Katsy from behind the wheel as she punches it again.

We hold on longer until the call comes that it is time to go back to port. "So wait, no one else gets to drive?" I ask.

"Sorry, we have to get you guys back for the show. You can bring it into the harbor if you want though. You just have to keep it under five knots."

"Thrilling," I reply.

I don't know it at the moment, but I will soon long for that cool ocean spray. We are leaving for Iraq in the morning, and as we sit around at dinner that night, we have hopes of an uneventful travel day. Katsy, however, isn't ready to move on to the next day yet.

"You like how well I drove that boat!?" she says, rubbing it in.

"If by 'drove' you mean 'filled with liquid,' then yes. You're a natural," I reply. "How about you go re-drive my coffee cup?"

"You're just jealous," she says. And I am a bit.

"It's cool. Just wait."

The room where we wait is 1,000° and it is constant. For 36 hours things have been tedious and stagnant in a way that only Iraq can be. We manage to get one show in at the Kuwaiti Naval Base before our itinerary is lost in an avalanche of unscheduled detours. Manifested on the wrong flight into Iraq out of Kuwait, we end up in Balad, a place we are not supposed to be until the end of the week. A quick nap later finds us waiting for a flight into our original destination, Kirkuk. Two shows have already been canceled, and after an unscheduled guerrilla set in the dining hall we get orders to fly again in the morning.

I remain baffled at why the country of Iraq is so hotly contested. I understand the oil argument now, but not the reason people ever managed to want to live here in the first place. It is alien and dry, with powdery brown dust settling on everything that isn't perfectly vertical. The hazy air is translucent tan at best, opaque at its worst. And the heat — dear GOD, the heat — is relentless. The thermometer will read 139° the day before we leave, though I doubt its accuracy to this day. How hot is that exactly? Picture making cookies, and going to the oven to check on them, and opening the door as that red-glow wave of heat singes your eyelashes. That moment right there? People live there.

In fact, I'm not even certain that the terrorists are terrorists at all. I sometimes wonder if those suicide bombers aren't blowing themselves up just to cool off.

So in Kirkuk that next morning, we wait. You fly at 0930 they tell us. Everything is always military time, which means automatically translating it in my head. If it's higher than noon, subtract 12. It is awkward. 0930 is now canceled they say. Just a few more hours. The air conditioner is broken. There might be a small fan somewhere but it is useless against the open door at the end of the room. The sun has banged away at the gates long enough that this building has simply given up. Just a few more hours.

Your new flight is at 1330, they say. The dust is too thick to fly in. Visibility is zero. They can't get the rotaries in the air with the sky like this. Even bubbly Katsy is beaten at this point; she lies motionless on a bench. In this heat, your soul cooks to medium well. 1330 comes and goes. 1700. The air is so thick that you can't see across the parking lot. We are nowhere near where we are supposed to be, and another scheduled show is canceled while we sit waiting. All we can do is wait, but the only thing that comes is more sun. Then, to our relief, the Blackhawks finally arrive.

Blackhawk helicopters are quite possibly the coolest pieces of machinery I've ever seen in my life. Through Iraq and Afghanistan, I've taken them everywhere. They look like sharks, if sharks flew in pairs and had massive guns hanging from their skin. At night the insides glow green and if you look hard enough through the darkness you can just barely make out your companion helicopter as it hovers out there in the black sky. The desert air, regardless of the time of day, slips hot through the open sides as you cut your way across the landscape. Occasionally, flares flash green and white as they break the lock of a radar down below.

As the rotors slice through the air, they generate a massive current that circulates clockwise. It whips downward and blows directly into the open back window on the right side of the chopper. It blows hard there. Very hard. It's a miserable fact I learned on my first chopper flight, and one I've never forgotten.

We eventually escape the base in Kirkuk and land at a forward operating base called Warhorse. An hour after landing we hit the stage. Outside and under halogen lights, the bugs swarm as we tell our jokes. A sea of soldiers in fatigues and reflective belts are laughing in front of us, making the dust and the waiting over the last few days worthwhile. I like these people, I think to myself. Good, says Life. Get used to them.

Three days later and we're still here. Another dust storm, another missed flight, another day in that godforsaken brown powder. The Shiite and Sunni can pretend that they defend the region for religious reasons, but at some point they would have to admit that no god, Allah or otherwise, has come anywhere close to caring about this hellhole for some time.

There is the dust, and then there are the flies. Lots and lots of flies. They hover and buzz and land on everything, their bodies sticking to traps in black masses, while thousands of others circle, still alive and hungry. I expect the river to turn to blood next, but the river is dry. I sit here, hoping a flight will leave before the other eight plagues hit.

We arrange an additional show at the DFAC, the dining facility, on Warhorse. Sometimes you hear stories from other comics about the flawless shows where everything goes exactly as it should and you step off stage to roaring applause and a standing ovation.

This is not one of those.

The ambient roar of 1,000 people conversing and the clanging rattle of contracted Iraqi nationals pushing metal carts of food swallows our jokes as quickly as they can limp out of a sound system that barely reaches 40 of the hundreds of sets of ears in the dining room. It is like screaming into a jet engine. Halfway through his set, Sam makes the comment that he deserves a Purple Heart for surviving the show. He knows that you can't end up in Walter Reed Hospital for wounded pride, but he still isn't joking when he says it.

Eventually they manage to schedule a chopper out to Warhorse to pick us up. My new best friend, a Sergeant Nethers, arranges a nice little diversion in the event that we are unable to get out after all.

"If the sand doesn't break, I've got you cleared to go out on an MRAP and shoot the .50 cals," he says.

"Who's shooting cows?" Katsy asks, wide eyed.

"We just met her yesterday," I say.

"I'm gonna get you, Slam Bam. Watch," Katsy shoots back, cracking us all up.

"I didn't forget about the boat, you know. You have one coming."

"Uh huh. Try it," she says, and we laugh some more.

Thirty minutes before we are supposed to follow Nethers out to shoot the .50 caliber, word comes that our bird is inbound. "Grab your gear," someone says. "You have to go. Now."

As I put on my vest, Katsy flies past me. She wants to be first on the chopper just like on the boat, I realize. Well, cool. How perfect, actually. I ease in behind her in the queue as the rest of the passengers line up. They open the door leading out to the helipad and we march out in single file. Only as we approach the chopper do I slowly move in beside her.

"Take that seat!" I yell over the wind and sand, and motion with my hand toward the back right. "I'll take the one facing backwards since I've flown before! You take the good view this trip!" I'm not completely sure that she hears me until she slips over into the seat that I'd indicated. She gives me a quick thumbs up.

"You're welcome!" I yell.

We buckle our four point harnesses as Sam and a group of soldiers pile in after us with their gear. We are packed in tight as we levitate off the pad and into the baking desert sky. "Your turn!" I say, and wink at Katsy.

At 150 mph, the wind tears into the cabin like a rabid dog. She tries desperately, hopelessly, to cover her eyes. Her cheeks vibrate as the burning air claws at her face. She squints and turns her head, but it is everywhere. It pries her mouth open and rips her gum from under her tongue where it hovers for a brief moment before bouncing off a soldier's helmet. She tries to bury her head in the corner but the hell-bent, gale force banshee still finds her. It rocks her back and forth and makes her skin quiver and flap.

I cackle across from her, my camera snapping picture after picture while I try not to hyperventilate with laughter. It is totally worth those wet blue jeans.

We will ultimately make it back to Kuwait in one piece and on time, but only after several unscheduled stops. We spend a day at a base dubbed "Mortar-ritaville", so named for the relatively ineffective daily shots lobbed over the wall by insurgents. We march up the ramps into c-130s and we fight the engines as they hum and push blistering air at us across the tarmac, all while that incessant sun floats like a molten penny in the haze. We sit huddled in our rooms waiting for the all clear after a warning siren at the final base. "Just wait for the boom," we are told. "If you don't hear the boom, it's not good."

"Wait, what's it mean if I don't hear it?' I ask.

"That means it hit you."

Climbing on board our flight back to DC, I am exhausted. As we draw close to the States, I watch a friendlier sun rise through the window somewhere over Newfoundland. At 35,000 feet, things fall into perspective. Staring down through the cobalt blue and orange tinted clouds I can make out the twinkle of city lights.

As people shake themselves awake seven miles below me, I wonder what they are doing.

Somewhere down there, someone is rushing to get to an office so they can yell at people for not pumping out enough of some trivial product or another. People are neglecting their families to race after a paycheck that will only buy more things that probably won't make them as happy as time with their family would have. From the air, it is so easy to see how worthless a lot of our efforts are. I remember hearing a story about a businessman and fisherman somewhere in Mexico, a story that I can't quite recall now, but that I am certain sums up my feelings as I stared out that window. I think the businessman was trying to convince the fisherman to work harder so that he could essentially get where he already was.

Then I think of the soldiers that we just performed for, and just how tough the conditions can be, not only for them but for their families back home in the States. I was out for two weeks and am completely worn out from the heat and the early mornings and the cramped conditions. What our soldiers have chosen to do, for years on end, makes them nothing short of amazing to me. They're heroes. Not just for their service, but for all that service entails. I barely survived a taste of it.

I don't know a lot of things. I don't know if our presence in the Middle East is good or bad. I don't know if it changes anything on a grand scale. The global aspect of our efforts over there aside, I know that I've met individuals that have made an impact on a personal level with the people of Iraq, and that's where it counts.

A real impact, too; not one that seems insignificant when viewed from a distance. I spend a lot of time wondering if I'm doing the right thing or if I'm in the right place or if I'm not supposed to be somewhere else with someone else doing something else. The one thing I get while staring out of this window is that it doesn't really matter as long as I'm happy.

There's a world where bombs go off and people carry guns and other people blow themselves up because God told them to. It's a world where life can end abruptly and without warning, and I don't want to spend any more of mine chasing something unnecessary and useless.

I am grateful to those men and women that put themselves in that situation so that I don't have to.

Hooah!

ANOTHER AMERICAN

I'm running late. I have a week to kill between shows in Guam and another tour beginning in Portugal, and rather than fly all the way back home for seven days, I've decided to spend it in Cambodia. I spent last night in he Philippines, however, turning a layover into an overnight stop and another passport stamp. In hindsight, I am kicking myself.

I drank until they wouldn't serve me anymore — which says something for Manila — in an attempt to brush off all the flying I've been doing. This morning came early, however, and now I am in the back of a cab on my way to the airport with a fuzzy head and squinty eyes. This part of Asia is less organized than, say, a Japan or a Korea. Traffic here weaves nebulously around itself, some lanes changing direction depending on who has the brassier pair. We zip from one side of the road to another, sometimes over a sidewalk or through a parking lot, on our way to the airport.

My driver is the single loudest human being I have ever encountered. Part Chihuahua, part town crier, he screams into his cell phone in Tagalog. The cell phone is unnecessary of course; everyone in the capitol can hear him. We are on a four-lane road and traffic is everywhere. Motorbikes and small cars, delivery trucks, pedestrians, everything moving in concert. It is a mechanical orchestra without a conductor, synchronized by hive-mind and operated by what I can only assume is The Force. It is a gumbo made of 10,000 different trajectories.

In the middle of this swirling jumble of vehicles, my driver suddenly decides he has to pee. It's not said in conversation as a verbal reminder to do it when we get to the airport. He just pulls the car over across three lanes of traffic and jumps out. I glance out the window and he is right there, unapologetically. I turn back around and start fiddling with my phone as a million waves of cars whiz and honk their way past us.

The door opens and he's back inside now without so much as a hand wipe, and I begin to flip through my wallet for exact change. I expect the stop to make me even later, but we are unencumbered by things such as stop lights, other cars, or lane markers. We cut through the traffic like a rabbit escaping into a rice field.

Airports in this part of the world are not as organized as I am used to either. Sometimes there is a security check before you even get in the first door. Lines form in strange places and you stand in them because there is nowhere else to go. Our tires squelch to a stop at the end of one of those random queues. I heave 300 *pisos* across the front seat, careful not to touch his hand, then I sling my backpack over my shoulder and open my door.

SCREEEEECHHHH!!!

Another taxi makes a right into the spot next to us just as I open it. The edge of my taxi's door rakes through a solid foot of metal on the incoming cab's passenger door and the look on the driver's face is pure hate. He looks like Ricardo Montalbán's assistant from Fantasy Island, if someone had spent the entire episode letting hyenas bite his relatives in the neck.

Lean into it, I think.

I jump out and start yelling, not even sure who is at fault but determined to look more indignant. Tatu fires back in Tagalog, and my driver steps out to yell as well. The entire back and forth barrage is absolutely incoherent to me. This is how dogs and cats must feel all the time. They don't know what anyone around them is saying, but they definitely know when they're being yelled at.

Tattoo gives me a look that says, "So what are you gonna do?" in any language. I throw my hands up.

"It's your fault!" I shout. "You're the idiot that drove into a parked car." I say it loudly, confidently, and then I simply walk away. I have no idea what I am doing. Am I responsible for fixing this guy's car? I am in a foreign airport by myself and my only ticket out takes off in under an hour. Old episodes of *Locked Up Abroad* keep flashing through my mind. I can't remember which punishment goes with which Asian country. Am I going to get caned, or John McCain-ed?

"I call police!" I hear from behind me, and then Tattoo's hand is on my shoulder. At 6'1" I am bigger than him by far, and I spin around glaringly.

"Do it!" I say, right in his face, and then I storm off again. Five steps later I come to a complete stop as I hit the end of the line to enter the airport. It is the equivalent of trying to angrily hang up on someone on a cell phone. Tattoo has gone back to his car and I am almost to the front of the line when a Filipino police officer comes up to me.

"Did you hit his car?" he asks.

"Absolutely not," I say. "My door was open and he drove into it." Only two more people stand in front of me before I am through the first security line.

The officer tells me he will be right back, and gives me a look before he walks off. I'm at the front of the line now and getting jostled. I realize that he said that *he* would be right back. He didn't say anything about me staying there to wait for him. I will plead semantics, I decide as I toss my bag onto the belt and race to the other side.

I never check a bag on a flight if I don't have to. I've lost too many to count, and I travel light anyway. In this case it is a blessing because I have my entire wardrobe at my side. I unzip it quickly, looking for something as drastically different from my black t-shirt as I can, but my bag is full of nothing but more black t-shirts. There is one bright orange hoodie at the bottom, but it is 95° in Manila today. Still, an option is an option. I also ditch my Jack Daniels baseball cap and throw on a beanie. I toss my sunglasses in my backpack despite my headache's protest. I might look like I am going skiing, but I don't look like the guy who just talked to the cops anymore.

Here is the good thing about racism. Sometimes it plays in your favor. I've never quite found it as racist as others do that people can't tell people of another race apart. We are spectacular with our own, but that's usually it. I can't tell Asians apart, unless one of them has a facial tattoo or a missing ear. I could tell you every single, subtle difference between Carrie and Beth in high school though. They were identical twins and I only liked one of them for some reason.

Everyone knows their own race while the rest of us look on mystified. There is probably something quite scientific behind it, but when a news broadcast flashes a wanted poster onto the screen, whatever "it" is, is the difference between, "Yeah, that looks like every black guy I've ever met", and, "Damn, Jay robbed that woman at the gas station."

But when it works in your favor, you don't think too negatively about it. My plan is to snag my boarding pass and then get lost somewhere past the second security checkpoint for good, but before I can complete the second part of that endeavor, I see the cop again. At least I think it's the same cop. See how that works?

He is glancing at the people in line as he makes his way down, and then he pauses when he gets to me. "Have you seen other American?" he asks.

"*Another* American?" I say in the heaviest, Russell Brand inspired British accent that I can muster. "'Fraid I can't help you there. I'm English, mate! Cheers!" And then, unbelievably, he lets me go right on through security.

And that's how the world works. No rules. Nothing hard and fast or written in stone; just people and physics, having near collisions and actual ones, and then careening off in new directions.

OCTOBER'S SONG

It is October. Which one doesn't matter; they're all the same. I have a morbid attraction to October for some reason. It is always ten months into the year when my life changes drastically, for better or for worse, whether I am ready for it or not. Each year I tiptoe into October's castle armed for battle, expecting one calamity or another to leap from behind a doorway and club my equilibrium to death. It is a forest full of rogues and robbers that I must pass through annually.

This year in particular I'm in Canada, waiting for the explosion.

I walk a mile to a coffee shop with the entire afternoon to myself. I stumble lost into the sunshine, under electric blue skies and across fields of green torn carefully from the pages of a children's book — a green punctuated only by the darting of coal black squirrels, dark as cigarette burns on a poker table. The colors are alive, popping and crackling in front of me, around the lake and into the woods, buckets of gold, green, red, brown, and yellow paint splashed on a blue wall.

The ducks float silently on the water's surface, toy boats headed nowhere in particular. They look bored. No, they can't be, I think. If they were bored, they would fly. I certainly would if I could.

It's not always bad, this October thing, but it's always significant. I've fallen in love twice in this cursed month, long stories each of them, though clearly neither relationship survived. I kicked my three-pack-a-day smoking habit at this point of the year as well, taking one last drag and then flicking the ember out into the Iraqi desert to smolder in what was, appropriately, one big sand-filled ashtray. My first paying gig on stage was in October. So was my first trip outside of the United States, and the beginning of my first time circumnavigating the globe.

But the good month giveth and the good month taketh away, and it's the "taketh" that roll through my head today. I'm sitting on the patio of this café watching strangers. How many of them are in here fighting their own personal battles, I wonder?

There are 19 others here right now: six couples, one family of four, and three others sitting alone like myself. One of those three is on his fourth cup as he reads his book. What possible reason could he have to be that awake? Never mind. He's pretending to read *Infinite Jest*. The book and the caffeine cancel each other out.

The two ladies are far more interesting to me. The first reads her paper and nurses a Diet Coke. I'm certain this has been a ritual of hers for more than a few years. The other lady is leaving even as I glance over at her, as if she waited way too long for someone who never showed up. I take another sip of coffee and stare out over the water.

October harbors terrorists, I remind myself, and they're not coming for these people. They're coming for me. On an October day a million years ago, my morning radio show shut down and the station chained its doors while I was on a trip through Mexico. I came home to find both my livelihood and my passion at the time had been unplugged.

Five years later, the club I built to take the place of the radio station closed too, this time not because of someone else's bad judgment but because of my own. My misplaced trust in a business partner with a cocaine problem struck in June, but waited another 16 weeks to sound the death knell. I was in this same Canadian city when the call came that my cats Athens and Izzy had died. When it wants to be, October is a hate-filled motherfucker.

As a child I used to love it. October always heralded the end of relentless Texas summers where the heat ignored any normal conception of seasonal change, and baked the ground through the end of September. It marked the beginning of the occasional crisp night and a chance to steal wildly through the neighborhood collecting candy from both neighbors and strangers alike.

Halloween was magical, even if our costumes were not. How my mother managed to clothe and feed four boys as a single parent on a school teacher's salary confuses me to this day. I have trouble keeping my own head above water sometimes. Still, we were a creative bunch, and a lack of pricey, store-bought costumes wasn't about to keep us from filling sack after sack with the sugary spoils of trick-or-treating.

We trekked as a unit — the Ghost, the Mummy, the Punk Rocker, and the Baby — the cost of our costumes totaling around a $1.50. A package of Kool-Aid, a roll of bath tissue, and a bed sheet got the job done somehow. It was a sad sight looking back on it. I lurched through the streets with my head wrapped in toilet paper, wearing blue jeans and a white button-up with the remaining 20 feet of tissue slung loosely over my shoulder or stuck to the bottom of one of my shoes. Jeremy had gone from rockstar to Smurf as the sweat mixed with his blue-raspberry-dyed hair-do and ran down his face.

My brother Brandon maintained his ghost persona for almost an entire 20 minutes before the sheet ended up in a ball under his arm. Because the sheet had to go back on his bed the next day, he wasn't allowed to cut eyeholes in it, which meant that after stumbling blindly over a curb or two and slamming face first into a tree, he would give up and carry his "costume" to the next house and try to pull it over his head before anyone answered. His difficulties were compounded by the fact that he had Star Wars sheets. It's hard to be scary with a Millennium Falcon on your head

Hunter, the youngest, had it the easiest. His Baby outfit was just him, a one-year-old lugged around behind his older candy-hungry brothers. He was too young to actually eat any of it, but as long as we carried him, we were also allowed to carry an extra bucket too. No one worried about razor blades or poison candy. Those were awesome autumn nights filled with pumpkins and candles and toothy grins. I cannot imagine ever looking forward to October the way I did back then. Not knowing what I know now.

More people are at the coffee shop now. They arrive as quickly as they leave. For most of them, this is just a minor waypoint on the long journey of today; for me it is reflection. The steam rises off the surface of my drink while October's song plays in my head. The cobblestone streets of Germany that I walked with wide eyes and an explorer's heart. Facing down the fear of standing on a real comedy club stage for the first time. Locking the door to my own comedy club for the last time. The deaths of friends and habits. The discovery of new ones.

Every year something different is added to the collection of paintings hung on my wall by this ridiculous month. I wonder sometimes if we make things like this happen. If I can say this without diving down some metaphysical rabbit hole, I think it's something subconscious that we do to ourselves, and it has a way of manifesting itself.

Am I obsessed with October because of what happens, or do the occurrences happen because I'm obsessed? Do other bad things happen in other months, or am I blaming October because a lot of them happened during its 31-day reign? It's possible that it's just the month of the Baader-Meinhof Phenomenon.

So maybe I do predispose myself to big things happening in October, good and bad. Maybe it's when I feel both the most empowered and the most vulnerable. I find it strange though, that all my big events happen at this exact point on the calendar, ten months in, in some vortex of luck and anti-luck.

The whole month is green and grey and black to me. The leaves change, the weather changes, and I change. For better or worse, every single time.

THE RECORD PLAYER

I am sitting outside at my favorite coffee shop; one of the last times I will do so before I move away from these sleepy streets of Beaumont for good. The man sits across the patio from me at a cluttered table in a puddle of sunlight and his own eccentricity. I have long since come to terms with how I am a divining rod for insanity. I can spot it in a crowd, and in some instances I am even magnetic. It doesn't wait for me to find it, but instead fights its way to the front. I've seen a lot of crazy people.

This guy though, this guy is a rare gem. A trucker's cap covers his balding head, which on its own is not unusual. He is also wearing a fanny pack and a tube top, however, and has eight mountaineering clips attached to his belt with nothing on them.

And he is carrying a record player.

It isn't my first encounter with this man. He is thin and frail, and I imagine that he lives as a stowaway in his mother's basement, occasionally trying on her clothes when she goes to work, and exploring the inner workings of his turntable. The first time we met, he cornered me on this very same patio and proceeded to discuss the different types of solder — the melted metal you use to stick other metal things together. It was more of a monologue on his part than an actual conversation.

"We used to use lead-based solder back when I was on the inside. Lead. Lead is good. Now everything's lead-free and useless. It's better they say, but it's not the same thing. It all depends on what you want to join. Sometimes I just put things together to see if they'll stick. Did you know you can't solder something to a mouse? Won't work. Not even with 18 gauge rosin flux. It runs. The mouse I mean, not the solder. Ask me anything about solder, and I can tell you."

I've learned since then to keep my earphones jammed deep in my ears whether I'm listening to music or not. It buys me the freedom to observe without participating. Today I watch, intrigued, as the man alternates between tasks, sometimes rolling cigarettes, sometimes strategically arranging the napkins on his table, and sometimes taking a moment to run his tongue along a lighter shaped like a deer's head.

This last fact is deeply disturbing.

Years ago, I used to make a habit of randomly picking up homeless people and taking them for fast food. I've always been fascinated with other people's stories. I'm a collector, and the vagrant population has more than most to add to my collection. You won't get an earful of inner-office drivel from them. You're not in danger of having to listen to them prattle on about their misbehaving children or how the neighbor's dog won't stop tearing up the flower beds. Their stories are never that mundane.

It was never unselfish. I in no way felt like I was doing some great service to these men. At best — even if they were starving to death — I was buying them one more day, and it was unlikely that they were going to figure things out in those 24 hours. A Sonic burger in exchange for the chronicles of another human being seemed like an acceptable trade to me.

More than anything, I grew curious as to whether or not these people were truly unstable and wild, or if some of it was just an act. One man I remember was named Big Chief. Over tater tots he regaled me with tales of removing himself from the grid on purpose. Crow's feet and thick lines cut their way through his face as he talked, making him look like a Fredrick Remington sculpture had shaken to life. His Native American roots came through audibly as well, his voice possessing the broken, yet soothing, cadence of his ancestors.

"They are watching," he said. He glanced repeatedly in the side view mirror as he talked. "If they knew where I was, I would be dead, and you too most likely. If I can be on a different car every night, they cannot catch me."

"You hop trains?" I asked.

"It is better that way. In 2002 the world will end, and only those of us with places to hide in the jungles will be safe. I have gold buried across the country, so when the economy falls, I will be ready."

"Gold?" I was a bit incredulous.

"And jewels." He pointed to his pocket, where I saw the metal spiral of a small pad of paper sticking out. "It is all in here. When I worked for the Secret Service, I saved every check they gave me. I was there when they shot Reagan. Every dollar I made went to buying precious stones and metals, and only I know where it is all hidden."

The world didn't end in 2002 though, and I never saw Big Chief again. I imagine him sometimes, hiding in the forest on the outskirts of some sleepy town as night falls, burying nuggets of gold and marking their locations in his tattered notebook.

When I was 18, I worked at a grocery store. A homeless man named Redbeard frequently hovered outside one of the entrances, begging quarters from soccer moms as they wheeled carts full of food to their suvs. It was a brilliant ploy, accosting these people with assertions of hunger when they couldn't possibly argue that they had nothing to give. I never understood why these customers were so quick to go to their purses rather than hand the man a bag of chips or some lunch meat from their carts.

We called him Redbeard not just because of his matted red beard, but also because of the invisible parrot that sat on his shoulder and gave him advice. There was a pizza place next door to the store, and one day I invited Redbeard to join me on my break. Over lunch the imaginary bird miraculously disappeared and a much saner man emerged.

I grabbed another slice of pizza. "You don't really believe there's a parrot on your shoulder, do you?" I asked.

"Of course not," he replied with a gleam in his eye. "But I do kinda look like a pirate, don't I?" And it was true. He did.

"Honestly?" he continued. "They won't give you anything if they think you can help yourself."

There was some obvious logic to his argument, considering that he was sucking down slices of pepperoni on my dime. That encounter, though, has forced me to take a longer look at the crazy people I come across, which is what I find myself doing on this coffee shop patio with the man I know only as The Record Player.

Like the vagrants before him, he somehow ended up with a name like a Batman villain. They should have their own line of action figures. Legitimately crazy or not, I can envision a metropolis filled with them; a world where Redbeard and Big Chief knock off banks while The Record Player scrawls cryptic riddles on construction paper and leaves them behind to confuse the cops, as they all idle away into the night in the back of a boxcar. If they are captured, their insanity pleas will be airtight.

My own past is not exactly devoid of crazy moments, and I can't help wonder if I, too, have been labeled the same way by much saner people somewhere in the past. Crazy is such a relative term anyway. What right do I have to sit here and judge this man? Maybe he continues to cross my path for a reason.

Perhaps it is even Life's way of keeping me humble. "Don't get cocky, Slade. Regardless of what you think about yourself, you're still one table away from a guy licking a lighter."

JEDI, STRIPPERS, WHISKEY, AND WORDS

"So the Death Star is the woman?" Sam asks.

"Yes! Finally! Someone else finally gets it. I've been trying to say that for half-an-hour," the stripper says. She has to be a stripper. I have been passively sitting at a table in the back room of the Laff Stop, sipping on a Jameson and watching this nuclear winter of a conversation for the past 20 minutes.

The Laff Stop comedy club was legendary before it closed, but that won't happen for another three years. Mitch Hedberg, Joe Rogan, Ron White, Louis CK, and Doug Stanhope all recorded classic albums there. Sam Kinison's piano sits behind a curtain in this room, unplayed for years by anyone other than his ghost. Bill Hicks worked out the ideas on the stage to my right that would ultimately make him an underground icon.

Open Mic Night happens in the front lobby of the club on Mondays, while the comedians clique up back in the main showroom, waiting for their turn on a five-hour night. It isn't just the pros; Monday nights attract an entire circus wagon full of freaks, all determined to take their shot under the spotlight and flick their strange coins into a human wishing well of unfamiliar faces. It's one of these nights that finds me in the middle, and inside a conversation I shouldn't be paying attention to in the first place.

The stripper is dressed to kill, and by kill, I mean if you look at her too long you will probably catch some disease capable of ending your life. She falls out of her clothes haphazardly, her un-toned rolls of flesh crawling out of a ripped pair of jeans designed for a much younger, much thinner girl. Her makeup has been applied with a paintball gun.

She wandered in like she was looking for crack and has now somehow signed up to tell jokes. In an effort to alleviate her fears, someone has told her that I am a first-timer too, but that I'm too scared to actually go up. Instead of bolstering her confidence however, she's decided to use that nugget of misinformation as a weapon. The only thing more amusing to a table full of comedians than watching a hopeful comedian attack a veteran, is watching a hopeful comedian attack a veteran and then prattle on about their own brilliant comedic theories, ideas, and jokes.

And that she does. In between firing shots at me, she explains to anyone who will listen how she has put to order completely unrelated events, the most current of which is her mission to explain the sexual intent of George Lucas in the *Star Wars* trilogy.

This is definitely the meth talking. She is a drunken plane crash, and I am unable to look away as her engine sputters and fails and a plume of smoke shoots out of the back of her descending aircraft.

"You're an idiot," I finally have to say.

"You're not even supposed to be back here. This is for comics!" she yells. "Go back out front with the rest of the audience."

"And please stop showing everyone your underwear," I add, ignoring her comment. "It's not attractive. At all. To anyone. Really."

"You're a dick," she says. "You're more than a dick — you're a fucking asshole."

"Dude, that's the longest a girl has ever had a conversation with you before calling you an asshole," Sam interjects.

"Shut it," I say. "Her vagina's still hanging out." I am talking indirectly about her, which I know is only making her angrier.

"Seriously, why is he still back here?"

"Because I want to learn to be funny like you," I say.

"You don't have what it takes," she fires back.

"If by that you mean a prison tattoo on my hip that looks like it was drawn on a Magna Doodle, then yes, you're right."

Sam interjects again, "I think what he was trying to say is that the whole idea just isn't funny. It needs, well, punchlines."

"Whatever. He doesn't know anything about comedy."

"You're right. I don't know anyth — Jesus Christ! What happened to your feet!?" Whatever point I was trying to make is erased instantly. Her feet look like they have been bound and beaten. Red marks wrap around the sides and her toes are crunched into a twisted point. It is confusing.

"I had to wear six-inch heels for a movie shoot today," she says.

"Porn?"

"No. For your information it was about this party where the women are topless and—"

"So porn."

"Asshole."

"Whore."

"Seriously. What do—"

"Seriously, what did happen to your feet? Your toes look like a T-Rex eating a pack of wieners."

While normally content to let me pick my own fights, Sam can no longer keep himself quiet. "What's worse than the Holocaust?" he asks. "Her feet."

"For real. You look like you've been playing hacky sack with a bag of gravel. Is that frostbite?"

"Oh my god," she says, staring at me with one of her crossed eyes.

"Here. Just take my shoes. You need them worse than me," I say. I start to unlace my Chucks as she changes the subject.

"What were we talking about?"

"*Star Wars*," Sam says.

"Right. So R2-D2 penetrates the Death Star with his metal 'arm' and then he—"

"You guys really aren't setting me up?" I finally ask, glancing around the table full of comics. "She's real?"

"I know," Sam reply. "I thought you were being *Punk'd*, but you're not famous enough."

The stripper can't handle the lack of attention. Positive attention anyway. "I'm *still* trying to make a point here!"

"Your feet *still* look like moldy ladyfingers."

"Can we leave my feet alone?"

"Look, you wore the sandals," Sam says. "You look like you were drunk and barefoot while trying to outrun a weed-eater." The stripper laughs at his reply, exhibiting no anger at all. I am surprised.

"Really?" I ask. "Why doesn't Sam get to be an asshole too?"

"Because he gets what I'm trying to say."

"Uh huh. What exactly are you looking at anyway?"

"What?"

"Your eye. Looking all this way and that."

"There's nothing wrong with my eyes!"

"Just one of them actually. It looks as if it just kind of gave up. It has a look of complete resignation."

"Whatever, asshole."

"Good one. You come up with that all on your own?" As I ask, another one of the pros comes into the back room, excited.

"Hey guys!" Ed says. He is clearly suppressing a smirk. "I just killed with this new bit about Darth Vader being a big penis and how the Dark Side represents the feminine spirit!"

"Oh my god!" the stripper says. "That's brilliant! We were just talking about that!"

"Shut up!" says Ed. "Seriously?" I kick him under the table.

"Yes. See?" she says, turning to me." You're the only one that doesn't get it, you dick. I could have you thrown out if I wanted to. Maybe you should go back up front until you have the balls to go on stage."

"And you should get a pedicure. And an eye patch," I say back.

"Actually, I think you're up next," Ed tells me.

"Enjoy your first time on stage," Sam adds.

"Yeah. Good luck, asshole," says the stripper. "Now. Where were we?" It doesn't matter. The comics are already up and headed back into the lobby with me, leaving the frustrated stripper sitting at the table by herself.

The problem with comedy is that it is impossible to ever really understand it. All the science in all the books in the entire world means nothing when it comes to what truly makes another human being laugh. Videos of people getting hit in the testicles by baseballs or small children are always hilarious, but why? We have no idea. A good joke is misdirection; a good comedian can take you by the hand and lead you down a road, and then suddenly change course on you to elicit a laugh. But again, why?

I have bits that I think are incredible but I can't figure out how to get them across in a way that works. On the other hand, I have lines in my own set that consistently do get laughs but I'm still not sure exactly why. How does it all work?

It's sorcery, if you ask me.

My goal this evening, as a supposed first-timer, is to bomb. There are nights when even the best comic can't manage to make it work with his absolute A-game, so eating it in front of people on purpose should be simple. In the few minutes before I go up I try to think like a rookie. Just do set-ups with no punchlines, I tell myself. Leave lots of silence. Die, on purpose. Gruesomely.

"So wow. Black people and white people are really different," I say, and then move on, giving no evidence in joke form. "So, uh, what else is going on?"

Every intentional nose dive brings more chuckles from comedians that know me, contradicting my attempt to flatline. The laughter grows steadily. Damn, this isn't the plan. I fight to keep a straight face as I stare out at the crowd. "Blank CDs suck," I pretend to stammer. "Especially on road trips." It is abysmal, yet somehow hilarious. I stare blankly ahead as more laughs come flooding towards me.

The stripper has migrated back into the room and I can see her glare from the stage. She is furious. I am a bit mad myself, that I haven't been able to pull off the ruse. My fellow comics have failed to play along. I am killing with non-jokes. Every misdelivered bit elicits an even bigger response. I am crushing. I couldn't do this well if I actually tried.

I finish the set to applause and wander off to the back room again, followed by a few comedians and the stripper. "There's no way that was your first time!" she says.

"You really don't get it," I reply.

"Seriously, how'd you do that?"

"I wouldn't tell you, even if I knew." And the truth is, I don't know. Even after all this time, comedy still confounds me. It works when it shouldn't and doesn't sometimes when I need it to most.

"You're such an asshole," she says.

As I walk away I can hear her voice trail off in the distance, still searching for an audience. "So has anybody else here seen *Star Wars*?" she mutters as the showroom door closes behind me.

FORMERLY PORCELAIN

We despise hecklers. If there is any confusion about that fact, I can confidently speak for every comedian who has ever held a microphone when I say that we hate them. If you are that person that can't help but "add to the show," we hate you too. As fun as it might look to watch a comic destroy a heckler, and as much fun as it might actually be for me to do it, when we do engage, we are simply trying to hellfght the fire so that we can get back to telling the jokes we want to tell.

I am in San Antonio this week playing a room that is essentially an aircraft hangar. It is a gorgeous room, but acoustically it is challenging. It is easy for a show to go off the rails here. I am hardly five minutes into my set, and the couple seated front and center hasn't shut up yet. The room is big enough that their chatter is probably lost on anyone but me, but I'm having one of those nights where my fuse seems easier to light than usual.

These two people simply cannot be the age they are. We're all getting older. All of us. Once we hit our mid-20s, I think we all begin to wish our lives would move Benjamin Button-like backwards. Instead, hair color fades like old construction paper and wrinkles zigzag their way through what was formerly porcelain. Most of us come to terms with this and gracefully own our new skins. These two, though, have placed no limit on what they will do to maintain their youth. Though they're both nearing 50, the man is the lesser evil in this pair. He is wearing the ugliest shirt I have ever seen with my face. It is all bright blue paisley and starched white cuffs with jalapeños embroidered on the inside. It looks like a casino floor, and it is unbuttoned half way, missing a very necessary undershirt so that the white chest hair sits like a greyscale velvet pillow beneath his gold chain. He is Larry from *Three's Company*.

The woman is a bigger mess. She hangs onto the last few days of her 40s by the fakest of fingernails. She has had every piece of plastic surgery done that a human being can talk a doctor into. If it can be nipped, tucked, tied back, stitched up, or botoxed, she has paid for it, and her breasts are faker than a soccer injury. The problem with plastic surgery is that they have never figured out how to fix the neck. It is the Holy Grail of the plastic surgeon, completely unattainable, so no matter how much landscaping is done around the dead body in the front yard, it is still there for everyone to see. Her neck looks like wicker furniture.

They have refused to stop talking to each other through what is now ten minutes of my show. I am distracted. I can see them. I look out into the crowd as I start each new bit, but they loom in my periphery. They're just talking, oblivious to me, this person with the microphone and the spotlight on him. Me. This person that they have, presumably, come to see perform.

While there is plenty of footage of me ripping hecklers to shreds, I don't like to do it if I can avoid it. Comedians are supposed to bring happiness, not ruin anyone's night. I will usually fire a warning shot over the bow when I catch someone being disrespectful during a show. I truly believe that most people simply don't realize how loud or distracting they can be. With a little slap on the wrist, they will pull themselves back together and watch the rest of the show like adults. Only when the situation calls for a scorched earth approach, will I take that tack.

I think that stand up has far more to do with crowd psychology than it does with actually being funny. Before you can get by with attacking someone verbally, you have to convince the audience that your target is a deserving one. You have to unify them against this villain. You repeat the things the heckler says so that the audience doesn't have to fill in the blanks. You remind the audience that distractions like this happen every day and that we are usually powerless to counter them. Be it an unsupervised kid in line at the grocery store, or the rumbling bass of an adjacent car at a stop light, or the neighbor who mows his lawn at seven in the morning on a Saturday, we are assaulted everyday by the unwanted sounds emanating from the selfish and uncaring, and we all long to lose our cool and shut those noises down.

This couple is one of those annoyances, unwilling to acknowledge that the rest of us are engaged in a common experience, and once I accept that they're not going to quiet down on their own, I loft out a line. It's not even a good one, really, but it's just enough to let them know that I can hear them.

"Wow," I say. "I didn't think there was any way you two could be louder than his shirt, but I guess I was wrong." It is a playful nudge to get back in line, and most normal people would fall silent about now and turn their chairs forward. Not these two. They get louder. I start another bit, but despite my effort to fall back in my rhythm, they are clearly not going to let me continue.

"Okay," I say, a little more frustrated now. "If you two are going to keep talking, there are 248 other people in this room, and we all want to know what is so important."

I hear a creaking sound as the woman looks up at me. Her neck sounds like a haunted house door. Rrrrrrrreeeccchkk! Her voice has the gravel of age in it. "I was explaining to him that the shirt you just made fun of costs ten times more than those ugly shoes you're wearing."

I am not concerned with her jab. My shoes are incredibly unimportant; I wear Converse almost exclusively on stage. I do however have to maintain control of the show. The words come out of my mouth so fast I don't even realize that I am the one saying them. I am a spectator of my own actions.

"Yet they still cost more than that horrible plastic surgery job someone did to your face," I say.

It happens so quickly that even I think, "Oh shit! Did you just hear what that guy said to you?!"

She loses it. Rrrrrrrreeccchkk! Her neck creaks again as she turns to the guy, who happens to be staring at me slack-jawed. "You better do something," she tells him. "We have been together for 30 years and you are just gonna let some asshole comic talk to me like this? This is bullshit! You better stand up and do something right now or I swear to God—"

And suddenly I am in the fray. My gloves hit the floor. "You swear to God what? Tell me? Watch this," I say, and look out at the crowd. One of my biggest weapons as a comedian is the ability to turn an audience on a heckler. It is the most powerful psychological arrow in my quiver. "By round of applause how many people wish these two would shut up right now?" I ask, and 248 people roar in unison.

I look back down at the woman now. "Do you hear that?" I ask. "*That* is what *hate* sounds like."

She loses her mind, screaming at the bewildered man sitting next to her. "30 years we have been together and you're just going to sit here while he talks to me like this? Get up and say something, you asshole! You kick his ass!"

"Stop it," I say to her. "Just stop. You're going to get him hurt. There are 248 people in here that can't stand you two, and the minute he stands up they're going to pile on top of him like Agent Smiths in *The Matrix*. Do you understand that?"

I watch the vitriol boil behind her eyes. She is not used to being talked to like this. She is usually the center of her world and she is befuddled. Her choice is to try to bring me down. I almost respect her for the attempt, but it goes nowhere. "You're not even funny! You probably do this because you can't get hired anywhere else, you asshole. And you're just mad because you can't afford a woman like me anyway. You don't know who I know, motherfucker. This is faaaaar from over. Just you wait and see."

I don't even interrupt her. I just let her wear herself out until she finally trails off like the end of a Lynyrd Skynyrd song. I let the room get eerily silent after she stops. You can hear the air conditioner as the entire audience waits to see what happens next, and even I am a little bit curious.

What does occur might be one of the cruelest things I've ever said in my life. "Look," I say, as I stare down at her with a hint of a smirk. "I'm sure you were pretty when you were young," which is heart-wrenchingly evil once you consider I have just called her both ugly and old before I even got to the comma. "So don't take this the wrong way," I continue, "but you look exactly like Bruce Jenner."

Keep in mind that this is way before there was ever a Caitlyn Jenner. I was referring to weird-looking-man-Bruce. Bruce 1.5, not the 2.0 everyone is so in love with now. The crowd winces as one, and I see her recoil like I've physically shoved her. She starts to yell again but I can't stop envisioning that face telling a Kardashian to go to its room.

Her fight is gone. Her sails flap windless and dejectedly. "Just go," I say, and she gets a horribly pained look on her face, or at least as much pain as you can generate with no nerve endings. She storms out as the crowd begins to cheer. I steal myself to continue the show when I look down and realize that the man did not leave with her. Instead first he stares up at me from his seat, and then as I give him my best "please just let this go" look, he starts to rise out of his chair.

Despite the unintimidating nature of his clown clothes, he is not a small man. "Whoa," I say, and reach back reflexively to grab the microphone stand, accepting that the crowd probably won't physically come to my defense after all and I prep to get at least one swing in before he mauls me. He gets all the way to his feet, reaches back, pulls a $20 bill out of his wallet, and sets it on the table.

"Man, I've wanted to say that same shit to her for 30 years," he says, and the crowd erupts as he bumps my knuckles and heads out to the lobby.

WHEN THERE'S LIGHTNING

Occasionally I go through periods where everything obscure that pops into my mind finds its way into reality. A conversation about an old neighbor from 25 years ago once led to an unsolicited email in my inbox from that neighbor's son a few days later. When I couldn't remember my third grade teacher's name, I asked my Mom, who promptly ran into her in a mall parking lot a week after our conversation. I think of things, and they happen.

Before I got on the plane for the Middle East in May of 2010, my friend Joe sent me a playlist for my iPod — a playlist that included Black Sabbath's *Mob Rules*. In the spirit of the song, I started a Facebook conversation taking pot shots at Black

Sabbath's lead singer on another friend's page, a friend who was a rabid fan. I've never disliked Ronnie James Dio, but it is hard to deny that he is easily made fun of.

And so we did. As a few of us took turns skewing his lyrics, I had to listen to more and more of his music for research, and as I did so, I found myself singing it in my head. *Holy Diver*, *Man on the Silver Mountain*, *Rainbow in the Dark*. It was my soundtrack as I trekked through the desert that week.

And then he died. I didn't even know he was sick.

The realization sunk in. I killed Ronnie James Dio. I did. Just by thinking about him. And now, on top of taking responsibility for his passing, I am forced to admit that despite years of arguing to the contrary, I was a fan. I really was. A latecomer — a convert literally the day before he died — but a fan nonetheless.

I don't know any of this yet, of course. Today is still years from 2010. Dio is very much alive, and I am on my way to see him perform with Black Sabbath in concert. I'm going with my friends Jared and Frenchy, along with five other guys whose names escape me, but they're not important.

What is important is Jared. Jared belongs at this concert, more than anyone possibly could. I show up in jeans and a t-shirt, the same way I show up to most places. Jared, on the other hand, has come to rock. He is a magician by trade, and dresses the part. The long hair, the flowing black shirt, the rings on every finger, and the bracelets — no, let's call them bangles — and the 12 necklaces, and the yellow sunglasses at night. He looks like Lorenzo Lamas on a shooting range.

His hair does not escape our group's alcohol-induced desire to pick on something. He ceases to be named Jared almost the minute we pull onto the freeway. He is Rapunzel, Mandy, My Little Pony, Chewie, a Highlander, and the worst episode of *Renegade* ever. We can't stop. Then come the Jesus jokes and the Bon Jovi references, and then the ridiculous.

Jared's hair is better than Winger. Jared's hair hit .350 for the Astros last year. Jared's hair beat Jif in a taste test 5–1. There are more Chewbacca noises and cracks about those godforsaken yellow glasses, plus side bets on how long he is going to wear them. Someone says something about BluBlockers and Bono, and there is the obligatory Corey Hart reference. "Good thing he has them on," someone says, "in case we need to locate DNA or find a lost golf ball."

Eventually, we make it to the concert venue where I fall out of the car in a fit of laughter, my side hurting as I fire off another crack about how cool it must have been to live with The Addams Family. I learn something tonight as we snag a few lawn seats and $12 beers, and catch the end of Megadeth's opening set. It isn't just Jared. Remember those people you made fun of in high school? Once a year, they all get together and go to a Dio concert. All of them.

Though I've always prided myself on the database of music trivia stored in my brain, my knowledge of Ronnie James Dio has never strayed too far from the classics. Tonight I am going to be treated to the rest. 17 songs, and every one of them has something to do with either mountains, or demons, or the sea, or more demons, or devils, wizards, or dragons, or a castle, or a castle on a mountain by the sea where there are demons and wizards. There are lots and lots of skulls.

And everything is off of the *Heaven & Hell* album.

"We're Heaven & Hell, and this next song is about Heaven & Hell and it's called … *Heaven & Hell*. We'll do some more songs you don't know after that from our *Heaven & Hell* album, and then we'll do a cover of a song that we didn't write, but if we had we probably would have called it *Heaven & Hell*."

At some point Frenchy and I wander off, the two of us the only ones in the entire venue not mesmerized by the lyrical game of Dungeons and Dragons being played out on stage. We try to find Jared again, but looking for a long-haired guy in a black shirt at a Dio concert is somewhat like that scene in *The Thomas Crown Affair* where all the duplicates were walking around with the brief-cases. Eventually we give up.

We spend the next half hour laughing like children at the show and texting Jared messages like "I'm going to lower the draw-bridge. BrB." and "Slade just got eaten by a dragon." Then we laugh at the lighting, and how the lighting director only has three buttons to control the onscreen video. On, Off, and Skulls and Flames. We also discover that you can sing Billy Joel's *Piano Man* to every Dio song.

When we run out of things to make fun of, we write our own Dio songs, and when we hit our threshold for that, we rename the band. The InDio Girls. Bel Biv Dio. Celine Dio. Riamond Dio. Dio Suave.

I leave having had an incredible time. I will fall out of touch with these guys I came with over the next few years, and I will rarely think of Dio again at all, at least until he passes away. And when it does happen, I'm sure he'll ride his tiger into Heaven or Hell, or wherever metal goes when it dies, but he will manage to capture one final fan on his way out the door.

I'm sorry I killed you, Dio.

JUST LIKE A WAVING FLAG

My love for world music is not a secret. While my default setting will always remain rock and roll, tribal rhythms and drum beats never cease to move me. I am inspired by the naturalness of it all, not always adhering to the Western verse/chorus/verse approach, and not always in a language I understand. It is bright energy captured by instruments and vocal chords.

I wish sometimes that I were capable of producing sounds like that, but I possess zero musical talent myself. None. At all. I own three guitars and a drum kit and I can't play any of them. I can play G, C, and D, and I fake the C because it's too hard to play the right way. My friend Kevin once brought me on stage to play the tambourine, and we have since struck an unspoken agreement that we should probably never, ever try that again. I apparently have the rhythm of a broken metronome. It's for the best I suppose, as

I'd hate to find out that I possessed a talent for such an instrument as the tambourine.

I would feel obligated to pursue a gift like that.

The tambourine has always intrigued me. I think my fascination began back when Nick at Night used to air old episodes of *The Monkees*. Davy Jones used to play his like a god. Sometimes it was as if he'd gone into a trance, the way Jimi used to do with his guitar, only Davy did it much, much better. Anyone can play *The Star Spangled Banner* on a six-string; try it on a bell-covered disc.

For almost a decade I dreamed of entering the Rock and Roll Hall of Fame as the tambourinist for a huge band. I fell asleep at night hearing Joe Elliot introduce me along with the rest of Def Leppard as we were inducted. After Rick Savage rumbled through a bass solo, they would get to me. "And on tambourine, from Houston, Texas, Mr. Slade Ham!" As I jingled the instrument that made me famous, the crowd would go wild, one person at a time, until the room couldn't hold anymore screams or applause.

I've let that dream go though, and not just because Def Leppard is never getting into the Rock and Roll Hall of Fame. I have a higher calling now.

World music is a vague term. Somewhere on the outskirts of that broad canvas is reggae, and in the center of reggae stands the Marley family. Bob sired Stephen and Ziggy and Julian and Ky-Mani and Damian, the latter of whom just happened to step onto the stage while I am standing in the audience.

And this is where my dream shifts. Goodbye, tambourine. I have a new hero.

His name is Garfield Logan. If you search the name on the internet, it will take you to pages dedicated to DC Comics' Beast Boy. If you go see Damian Marley in concert though, you'll see someone much more impressive than a superhero. The real Garfield Logan, sometimes referred to as Judah or Donovan, is a dreadlocked monument to perseverance and dedication, and a man dangerously capable of stealing the spotlight from anyone he steps on stage with.

Damian is performing with rapper Nas on their *Distant Relatives* tour, supporting a record that is half hip-hop, half reggae, and full of driving rhythmic beats, bass lines, and addicting choruses. The live show would still be amazing if it were just the two of them on stage, but they are touring with a complete band, including two guitarists, a bassist, a full drum kit, bongos, backup singers, dancers, and a pair of keyboardists. So which role does Sir Garfield Logan play? None of those.

He waves a flag.

That's all he does. As Damian and Nas walk out of the wings and into the center of the stage, they are followed by a Rastafarian flag so big it could be at a car dealership, whipped side to side by the 6' 6" Garfield. Not passively the way an old person waves a little handheld flag on the Fourth of July, but with pride. Aggressively, exhaustingly, he thrashes the huge red and gold and green banner from left to right.

What a great way to start the show, I think. It must be tiring to swing that thing back and forth for a whole song. It looks like a swimming pool cover. Then the second song begins, and the third, and the flag never stops. As the musicians riff through reggae beats infused with Ethiopian jazz, he marches back and forth across the stage, the colors sweeping in bigger arcs with every song. I stand mesmerized in the front row.

The first hour passes and he never slows down. He looks possessed, some *Serpent and the Rainbow* zombie on a flag-waving mission. If he has pupils, they are gone. Pure white eyes flash like a *Mortal Kombat* character or a snake that has recently turned into a human. He transcends reality. 90 minutes pass. 100. The flag ripples through the air, left and right, harder than ever before.

The son of Bob Marley sings clear and strong on the stage in front of me, yet I can't take my eyes off the madly whirling Judah and his flag. He brandishes it like it can do magic. He is a leader, hypnotist, puppet master, and bright white light all at once, floating through pulsing beats and Jamaican patois.

A thousand of us cross the two-hour point together and the show rattles to a close. As *Could You Be Loved* ends, Nas and Damian shout good night and walk off stage. The band plays the final notes as Garfield Logan stands spinning his flag in ever shrinking circles, until the flag rolls itself up in perfect sync to the music.

I stand inspired. Anything is possible again. It might take two decades of not cutting my hair, copious amounts of weed, and the upper body strength of a silverback gorilla, but I might get to be a rockstar after all.

I just need a band that needs a flag waved.

Long live Garfield Logan.

THE BIRD MAN'S SANDWICHES

It is the fly that gets to me. Flies don't like the cold, and it is down to around 60° in the room where I sit, forgotten and waiting. The police picked me up at my house five hours ago, and I still have not been processed.

"It's so mu'fuckin' cold," the old man says. He rocks back and forth on the bench and mutters that mantra every 30 seconds, as if he can raise the temperature just by describing it over and over again. He is a disheveled mess. His face is wrinkled deep like an Ansel Adams photograph. A few rogue teeth break through his gums like crystalline formations on an alien planet. Stains and dirt cover his shirt and I can't help but wonder what he had been doing right before he was thrown in the back of a squad car. My guess is that he is homeless, but then again, in jail everyone looks a little homeless.

"It's so mu'fuckin' cold, man." The fly lands lethargic on my arm as another batch of men are escorted in.

I keep saying that I am not a huge proponent of violence, but my past is riddled with examples to the contrary. I grew up in a household with three brothers. Very often a conflict would be resolved in favor of whoever inflicted the most pain. Even if we weren't arguing, we would wrestle and spar. The occasional dislocated joint or bloody nose or black eye was as commonplace as a plateful of rolls at the dinner table. I've grown up substantially since those rough-and-tumble childhood days, but traces of that kid remain lurking under the surface.

A week before my trip to jail, I pop into one of the local open mics on my way home. A few comedians are gathered outside in the parking lot. I slip over to say hello, not noticing that my friend Chase is standing stealthily on the fringe of the group holding a lemon pie.

If you've never hung out with comics before, you should know this: they are almost always up to no good. The presence of a pie crust full of meringue at two o'clock in the morning *never* means dessert. It means someone is about to take that pie to the face. I turn to say something to Chase and he smacks me. No warning, not even a real reason, there is simply a pie and a face that crept too close to it. It's just that it happens to be my face.

The lemon cream has not even begun to drip from my chin when the camera starts flashing. Al, the guy holding the camera, is not a friend of mine. On the contrary, he is one of a small list of people that I utterly despise. He isn't snapping pictures for a fun-filled PowerPoint look back at the goofy moments in my life. He is more than likely going to use them in a Photoshop project where large black men stand naked in a circle around me.

When I ask him to delete the pictures, he simply holds the camera up and displays a blank screen, having obviously flipped the camera to a different setting or directory. "They didn't take," he says, as if I am some sort of monkey-child with a learning disability. I know better; Sam and I pulled a similar trick on a security agent in an airport in Yemen a year ago. Al then switches the camera off and, as agilely as he can manage, darts off and jumps into his friend's truck, taking one last, quick second to lean out of the door and flip me off before slamming it shut.

Suddenly I am 12 years old again and my brother has tossed a final insult at me before attempting to close himself safely in his bedroom. I shoot to the truck door, jerk it open, and pull the camera from his hand. As I power it back on, he leaps out after me and grabs me from behind. The teenager instincts remain, though they struggle with the adult half that is pleading with me to be responsible. "Let go of me, Al," I say.

I repeat that three times. Finally I spin around and punch him. It isn't hard, just a jab really, but it is well placed and enough to knock him back. "I told you," I say, and then I launch his camera

50 yards across the parking lot. It is childish and irresponsible, but it is 100% me. I go home and think absolutely nothing more of it.

"We have a warrant for your arrest for misdemeanor assault and criminal mischief," the detective says. I glance around looking for the television crew. I am obviously being set up, right? "We need you to come downtown with us." Charges have been filed and I am being brought in for them. I will assume that most readers, like me at one point many moons ago, have never been in back of a police car. They are not luxury vehicles. The seats are hard, molded plastic. There is absolutely zero leg room, and it is almost impossible to sit in any sort of a comfortable position. Were it not detrimental to the gas mileage, I have no doubt that they would have carved them out of granite. It is so uncomfortable in fact, that being in jail actually feels like a relief. Fortunately, the officer appointed to drive me is a fan of my friend's radio show, on which I am a recurring cast member.

"Oh wow," Officer Nguyen says. "You're *that* Slade. Nice to meet you." And with that he rolls down the back windows for me, turns up a rock station, and we cruise to the Harris County Jail while Paul Rodgers — of the ironically named band, Free — sings *Alright Now* through the speakers.

I am pretty sure the fly is dead, frozen on my arm. It doesn't even move when I try to shake it off. It just sits there, stuck, reminding me of my fate. That fly is in for life. He has given up. I am only in for the night at the most, but the fly's hopeless surrender is beginning to get to me. For two hours we sit motionless on the same bench, through an employee shift change, and through several batches of freshly dropped off criminals. I still haven't been processed yet.

"Y'all know it's mu'fuckin' cold in here," the old man repeats one last time before being dragged to a cell.

Over the next few hours, I am led from one painted brick room to another. Wait here. Go there. Hands behind your back. Fingerprints are taken along with my photo, and a less than enthusiastic jailer calls me a "dumb motherfucker" when I try to pull a repeat of my Dragonslayer-as-an-Occupation ploy. "I ain't got time for this shit, you dumb motherfucker," she says. "Your job is 'none'. How you like that shit? Now turn to the left."

"Fine. Just write down Comedian." I say.

"Oh, now you's a comedian?" She cocks an eyebrow at me before yelling over her shoulder, "Hey everybody! We gots a comedian up in this bitch!"

"I'm serious."

"Sit down, you dumb motherfucker," she says. I stare blankly at her as I try to figure how, out of the two of us, I am the one in jail. I am led down another long concrete hallway to an elevator, where I am placed behind a metal screen to protect the elevator operator. I wonder briefly if I am being transported to Con-Air as the lift clangs to a stop and another jailer escorts me onto an upper floor.

"You're in here," the man says. I turn to face my temporary home. It is a white room, empty except for a metal table, a trash can, a toilet, and two other occupants. A blonde man sits on the floor in the corner, while a wiry black man — Bird Man, as he will later introduce himself to me — perches on the table scratching his arms and furtively glancing around at the ceiling. He is obviously in for crack.

The white guy is a different story. He just sits sullen and silent, his eyes little more than sunken hollows behind the filthy hair that hangs in front of them. He wears a white Sherwin-Williams t-shirt, but I am not completely convinced that the deep crimson blotches that cover his clothes are paint. If they are, he was arrested in the process of very carelessly painting a blood-colored room. Even if he didn't kill someone earlier tonight, there is very little doubt in my mind that he has done so before.

"Who wants a sandwich?" Bird Man asks. He shoves a crust of bread past his teeth as he talks, the crumbs bouncing down his mouth and chest like a landslide. One hand scratches aggressively at his neck. "There's another one here somewhere." He pops off of the table top and heads to the trash can, reaching inside and pulling out another sandwich.

"They're everywhere. Want one? There's more where that came from, yep yep." I sit down on the bench attached to the table, as far from either man as I can get. I pull my cap down over my eyes and try to look asleep. I immediately feel the table move. Lifting the bill of my hat, I see Bird Man's wide grin tilting left and right as he stares at me. He is crouched on the table top again. "Sandwich? We got sandwiches. Did I ask you already? Sorry. It's just that they're so good, these sandwiches. Best ones yet." He scratches and scratches at invisible bugs on his arms and neck while he makes his pitch.

I privately hope that the murderer will get up and kill Bird Man for his food.

Eventually my bond paperwork is processed and my name is called, though being cleared to get out and actually getting out are two different things. The government is incorrigibly inefficient at everything always. Even on a municipal level, taxpayer dollars are used as ineffectively as possible. In the final room before freedom, those of us on our way out are left to wait patiently for our property so that we can be discharged.

20 minutes pass. 30. 45. Chris sits across from me in this purgatory. I know his name is Chris because he has it airbrushed in huge letters across his shirt. There is also a picture of his truck next to a waterfall. Someone must have given him a gift certificate to one of those mall kiosks for a recent birthday. His patience runs out before mine does. "Why are we still here?" he yells at the barred window. "You can't keep us locked up like this if we're cleared to go, man. Now I know why those tigers be biting motherfuckers in zoos."

The lady on the other side of the window is completely desensitized. She doesn't even look up. "Waiting on your paperwork to get here. Have a seat, sir."

"How long's it take? It's been an hour. Y'all don't have email? What'd they tie it to a pigeon's leg or something? Jesus H Christ, lady. Shit, motherfucker, damn."

I try to ignore his yelling while I reflect on the fate of the fly. It seems like an eternity ago that it settled defeated on my arm. Someone should let that fly out for time served, I think to myself. Of course he'll have to wait another day for them to release his property and I'm not entirely sure how long flies live.

Eventually I make it out and have to go through a series of court visits to resolve the matter. I am supposed to learn that you can't hit people you don't like, and that there is a system in place to punish those who violate society's basic tenets. I leave with none of that however.

I don't like dirty places and I certainly don't like confinement or inconvenience, but I do like to watch people. I got to go behind the glass and hang out with the circus and ponder my decision while sitting in the ring with the carnies. Between Bird Man's crack addiction and the Painter's probable murderous spree, what I did seemed pretty tame — honorable, even — and I'm expected to be sorry but I'm not. If I'm to be perfectly honest, I think that sometimes a good right hand can resolve a problem far more quickly than months of red tape and paperwork and bickering lawyers ever could.

EVERYBODY HURTS

"If I'd known I was going to end up here, I would have hit him a lot harder and way more than once."

You can't say that to the people who work in the probation office. I want to, but I also want to go home, and that will most definitely prolong the process. Instead, I sit silently in the waiting room, watching the most inefficient system ever devised attempt to process a room full of "criminals."

At the Harris County Community Supervision & Corrections Department, they take pride in spreading the tax dollars they receive as thinly as possible; translucently thin in places, hiring 20 people to do a job that should take four, with none of them actually doing anything. There is a sloth-like receptionist behind a two-inch-thick glass window who puts everyone into the system when they arrive. The line snakes down the hallway, moving only when she does, so we drip past her window and into the waiting room slowly, like cold honey.

I am about to get an offender ID card, receive my community service assignment, and get evaluated to see if I need alcohol or drug counseling in addition to my already established probationary terms. "Go wait in the room until they call your name," the lady says once I finally get to the window.

There is more than one room, and I have three different things to take care of. "Which one of these do I do first?" I ask.

"Go wait in the room until they call your name," she repeats. It is the same intonation and tenor as the first time, machine-like and soulless. I turn away from the window as she clacks at her keyboard, puts the next person into the system, and mutters her mantra over again. I follow handwritten, misspelled signs down the hallway to a room labeled "iD cArds" and sit down to wait.

The walls are covered in anti-drug propaganda — a poster with trivia about pot, one of a crime scene chalk outline made of cocaine, the obligatory egg frying in a pan. In addition to the posters and the flyers and the brochures, they have also set up a television in the front of the room, like we are all third graders again with a hung-over teacher. "Just watch the movie," some lady says when she passes through to drop off a fresh stack of "Why you shouldn't do heroin" pamphlets.

The movie isn't a movie at all. It is a state-produced public service announcement about the dangers of drunk driving. I try not to watch for the first half-hour, but as time ticks on and my name remains uncalled, curiosity takes over. It is five minutes and twenty seconds long, the exact length of R.E.M.'s *Everybody Hurts*, which someone cleverly (as cleverly as the idiots who make these sorts of films can get) chose as the soundtrack, and the whole thing plays on loop. The never-ending arpeggio is being chiseled into my head with a dull spoon. An hour passes and the video just keeps replaying.

> *When the day is long*
> *And the night*
> *The night is yours alone*

The video itself sucks me in as well. I can't take my eyes off of it. It is like a car crash, probably because the entire thing culminates in a two-minute-long car crash. The film begins with groups of people out with their friends, all in different, innocent settings, some at a birthday party, some out with co-workers at a suburban Chili's, and some leaving a softball game.

As Michael Stipe sings, the scenes all become predictably similar. In each one the main character pantomimes shrugging off one more drink, and one-by-one their friends peer pressure them into a second or third beer or shot. It isn't even close to reality, and a brain-dead lab rat could see where this is heading.

> *When you're sure you've had enough*
> *Of this life*
> *Well, hang on*

Next comes the unsurprising introduction of the inevitable victims: a cheerleader leaving school, an old man crossing the street, a station wagon full of kids. Everything is going according to plan. I expect the standard, poorly-produced montage of all of them leaving at the same time, the screen fading out, and white text on a black background explaining how drunk drivers kill so-and-so many people a year.

Instead, everything explodes on screen. It becomes a Jerry Bruckheimer production, a Michael Bay-directed PSA, the must-see movie of the summer! Don't miss *Unnecessarily Violent Propaganda to Make a Stupid Point*, in theaters this summer.

The office worker's car spins as it rounds a curve. It bounces and flips once, twice, three times, like a gymnast. It slams into a tree and is whipped around. The passenger flies through the windshield, lands in the street, and pops like a water balloon full of meat.

The second baseman from the softball team rockets through a small-town road. The old man begins to limp across. The car rips around a corner. The man keeps moving, inching his walker along in front of him. The camera cuts back to the softball player, then the senior citizen again, back and forth, back and forth, then SLAM! The car blows through the old man, sending him cartwheeling over the top of the roof. The effects are amazing! I wonder if they haven't killed a few real people just to make this point. The government isn't above that.

I blink and miss how the cheerleader dies, but I look up to see her crumpled in a heap in the middle of a dark city street. R.E.M. keeps right on playing.

Everybody hurts!
Don't throw your hand, oh no!

BOOM! CRASH! EXPLOSION!

Don't throw your hand!
If you feel like you're alone!
No, no, no! You are not alone!

A mother cries in the hospital as a doctor shakes his head. The cheerleader blinks one last time. Some guy sprawls broken in an ambulance. Dead kids cover the front of another driver's car like love bugs. The station wagon burns. Sirens flash, lightning crackles, flashlights bob up and down in a smoky forest. That stupid song keeps playing. And then it simply fades to black and starts over again with the melodic D chord and a birthday cake.

As Hour 2 approaches, I finally make it in to get my ID card. An angry woman snaps my picture and sends me back to wait in the room again. I glance at the clock. My parking meter is about to expire and I am pretty sure I'm not even close to finished.

I walk back to the receptionist's window. "I'm going to feed my meter," I say.

"Go wait in the room until they call your name."

I cross my fingers that my name won't pop up in the 20 minutes it will take to go refill the meter, but based on the first part of the day, there is no real danger.

A different woman calls me to her desk after a half hour. "Go to Computer #5, start with Question #1, and come see me when you're done." It is my alcohol and drug evaluation. I am supposed to answer the questions honestly, and then a "specialist" will evaluate my answers to see if I need to take a class.

HAVE YOU DONE ANY ILLEGAL OR ILLICIT DRUGS IN
THE LAST 30 DAYS?

HOW FREQUENTLY DO YOU USE ILLEGAL DRUGS?

DOES YOUR DRINKING OR DRUG USE CAUSE YOU TO
HURT OTHER PEOPLE?

Are they really catching people this way? Probably. I click the
appropriate answer to all the questions, including:

SHOULD YOU WATCH FOR CHILDREN WHILE DRIVING
THROUGH A NEIGHBORHOOD?

SHOULD YOU PUT A GRENADE IN A BABY'S MOUTH?

and

WOULD YOU LIKE TO GO DIRECTLY TO JAIL FOR YOUR
ANSWERS?

I submit my responses, naïvely expecting a quick resolution to
this part of the process so that my parking meter doesn't run out a
second time. Instead, another hour rolls by before I get called, not
for the evaluation, but for my community service assignment. I'm
not yet aware that they issue you a specific place to serve your hours,
which completely screws up my plan to get out of doing them.
"You'll be working at the shelter, helping spay and neuter the animals," the woman says.

"I'm allergic," I spit out.

"To dogs and cats?"

"To everything." I realize that might not be the worst assignment I could get, but like many contestants on *Let's Make a Deal*,

I am cashing in my envelope for whatever is behind the second curtain. There are no take-backs. I instead end up assigned to The Center for Multicultural Awareness Through the Arts. Fuck. There must be a more tactful play than the one I have just made. "Maybe I could just take some allergy medicine and go help snip the dogs?"

"Um, no. That's your assignment. Go see Ms. Garza," she says. "She'll finish up your evaluation."

Ms. Garza's office is cluttered, and no one is in it when I arrive. I sit down at the desk and wait. I hear a clattering sound coming down the hallway, like a room service cart with a bad wheel. The sound, it turns out, is the sound of Ms. Garza's crutches as she goes from room to room. She has cerebral palsy, and has clearly just finished a stint in the hospital. A recent tracheotomy hole is almost healed, and her speech is an effort.

"So ... I've looked ... over your evaluation and ... I've determined that you need," she wipes a drop of drool away. "You need ... no additional counseling."

No shit, I say to myself.

"It says here ... that you have a ... Criminal Mischief charge ... So what did you do?" She painfully signs the forms in front of her, her body working hard against every one of her intended actions. I tell her the story, the brief version, of how I had punched a guy because he wouldn't let me go, and how I threw his camera afterwards.

"And he ... called the police?" She catches another drip of spit with the back of her hand before it hits her desk. "Wow ... he's a crybaby."

I begin to laugh. I suddenly don't care if I end up with a parking ticket. It has been worth the entire wasted day, and as many tickets as they can write me, just to hear a woman on the verge of physically falling apart call that kid a crybaby. Maybe I don't need to have hit him any harder after all. "Have a great day, Ms. Garza," I say as I leave, smiling.

"Oh, and you have a great day, too!" I say to the woman behind the receptionist's glass on my way out.

She doesn't even look up at me. "Go wait in the room until they call your name."

ON DEFENDING
THE HOME FRONT

Twenty-three. That's how many families they've paraded through my bedroom over the weekend. I have lived in this house for a year and a half; my roommate has been here much longer than that. The landlord has just filed bankruptcy however, which puts my living situation in jeopardy. A trustee has taken over the property and hired a real estate agent, who has proceeded to book appointments at her leisure, unconcerned that at least one person actually works out of this house.

Me.

And that is unfortunate for her. I wouldn't even give the real estate agent in question a name if I didn't plan on including dialogue. It's hard to write a conversation without a character having a name though, so I'll come up with something subtle that just sounds like her name. It rhymes with Janet Webster.

See, I am not in any way going to be the beneficiary of a quick sale of this house. I like it here but, unless the new owners are simply buying it as a rental, I am going to have to leave once the transaction is complete. I've never tried to sell property — I've never tried to sell anything really — but I imagine that like most sales people, realtors are heartless sacks of no-soul who are pretty much just after their 6% as quickly as they can get to it.

This one is anyway.

I get home on Friday to find the front door unlocked, the curtains over my bed slung haphazardly to the side, my shower door open, and my sandals kicked under my bed. Apparently the house has been shown to a family of drunken ogres. I kind of wish I'd been here to see it. Instead, I get to come home and clean up after them.

I call Janet to express my unease at having people go through my things, and to see if we can work out a showing schedule that allows me to be here when strangers are wandering through my house.

"I do not have to ask your permission to do anything," she says.

"Excuse me?" I reply. "I live here."

"Right now, yes. I'm in charge of selling the house though, and you can't stop me from showing it."

"I'm not trying to stop you. I'm trying to work out a better arrangement."

"I don't think you understand," she says. "I can show the house any time I want to until eight o'clock at night and you're going to have to deal with it. And when it sells? You and your roommate are going to have to move, most likely on very, very short notice."

"Ma'am, I wasn't starting a fight. What if I slow it down for you? I just ... don't want people ... here ... unless I am ... also here."

"I am not going to be talked to like a child—"

"Then stop acting like one."

"—and I will not be dictated to by some, some, arrogant tenant who—"

"You're acting like a child again, Janet."

"I am showing that house whether you're there or not."

"Well, now I think it's you who doesn't understand. I live here. I can be here all day if I need to be, and now it looks like I need to be. I was trying to work this out, but I can be a difficult mother-fucker to try to show a house around if I'm not in the mood to play nice. So here's what I suggest. I suggest you take your wittle bitty sign and you wittle wock box with the key in it, and stop acting like an uppity bitch."

"I am not going to be talked to like that!"

"Yes you will. Look, see? I'm doing it right now."

CLICK.

Then I immediately dial her boss.

"I have never been talked to like that in my life," I say. "She told me that I couldn't stop her, and that if I tried to call someone and complain, she would say that I said all kinds of horrible things. I'm not like that! This really, really hurt my feelings." If I could fake-cry, I would right now.

"I am so sorry sir. She can definitely be a bit brash sometimes, but that is totally unacceptable. I apologize on behalf of our company for her actions."

"It's not your fault. I look forward to an apology from her. Thank you so much for your time."

Home. The dictionary has its definition for it. It's far more than simply where you live. There are all sorts of clichés about the difference between a house and a home and all that other fuzzy feel-good stuff. I have no idea what it means. When you travel as much as I do, though, home is definitely more than just where you sleep at night. From hotels to condos to friend's couches or guest rooms, sometimes on an airplane, sometimes in the passenger seat of a car, it's definitely more than that.

That's why I am so attached to this house. It is the first place I have really felt settled in a long time. I have lived in five different places in the previous 12 months, though I have fonder memories of some more than others. I lived with my brother Jeremy for several of those months immediately following my father's funeral. I remember quite a bit about that place.

For instance, the porch at my brother's house had 25 boards that made up the floor, ringed by 63 smaller pieces of wood and topped by a flat board that was exactly the width of one-and-a-half lighters. There was a flower pot that measured four-and-a-half lighters tall, and there were 167 rocks in the flower bed around it. Those are details you learn when you lock yourself out of the house for four hours.

Shut up. It could happen to anybody.

I think the door was mad at me because I woke up earlier than usual. Normally it got woken up when my brother and his wife left in the morning and then got to go back to sleep for a few hours, but I happened to get up around 7:30 or 8:00 that day.

I intended to relax a little bit on that porch, so I shot to Starbucks, grabbed a cup of coffee, set it down outside, and then walked back inside to stash all the unnecessary stuff I was carrying. I kicked off my shoes, and stepped back outside to finish a phone call, with the best intentions of spending a very productive afternoon writing. All I needed was my laptop and my phone charger, and I probably wouldn't have to get up again for hours.

Enter the Door. I actually heard it say, *Not today, motherfucker.* And then it laughed that deep, evil laugh that doors laugh when they're angry. If you haven't heard it, don't worry. You will. There are variations on the theme. Car doors are the hyenas of the door world, laughing often and for little reason, but the house door is their king, waiting until the moment is right, locking itself rarely but strategically.

And there I was staring at it.

My immediate thought was that I had nothing to worry about. Even when I couldn't track my brother down, I still knew that I was more than capable of breaking into a house. My MacGyver knife was in my car and I trust my lock-picking abilities. It should have been simple, until I realized that I would have to circumvent the lock on my own car to get the tool I needed to get past the one on the house.

Slowly the realizations hit me. I had no shoes, so walking anywhere far wasn't an option, plus my wallet was in the house as well. My phone battery was flashing one fading bar, so it was hardly an asset either. I immediately started counting cigarettes and doing quick math; if I had eleven and my brother wasn't going to get home for at least four hours, I could have one every 21.8 minutes. How much $\frac{8}{10}$ of a minute was, I didn't know, but I had all afternoon to figure it out.

A quick check of the windows drove the point home. I wasn't going anywhere. This was my Apollo 13 capsule and I was stuck in it. Start rationing. Keep looking for a way out. There was an old coke can on the road that I could tear into strips and beat into a lock pick with two of the 167 rocks I had yet to count. Aluminum is not as strong as one would think, but I must have looked amusing clanging rocks together like a chimpanzee on the porch.

In hindsight, climbing fences, banging rocks, and counting boards probably looked a little weird to anyone passing by. I had to look legitimately retarded when taken out of context. "Awww, Jesse look. They're taking care of a 'special person' across the street, and they're even letting him play outside. I hear sunlight is good for the disabled. That's so sweet. Look at him banging away at those stones. He probably thinks they're drums."

I had officially passed the point of no return, and much like an airplane that had used over 50% of its fuel, I had committed too much time and effort toward resolving my situation to do anything other than resign myself to going the duration. I counted things. I stared at the roof. I did three pushups, before remembering that I don't exercise. I got excited when they delivered a phone book because I finally had something to read. I made it through most of the As. I talked to my feet, an expectedly horrible conversation. I drank the rest of my cold coffee. I figured out that $\frac{8}{10}$ of a minute is 48 seconds. Take that Mrs. Noblitt. You said I sucked at math and should focus on Art class.

I was ready to put notes in bottles and throw them out into the street. It was only four hours, but in my imagination, I had been stranded on that island of a patio for years, talking to a volleyball, dreaming of rescue. I was slowly losing my mind.

Eventually my brother came home, and I found the strength to reintegrate myself back into the real world.

But I'm not at my brother's house anymore. I am at mine, and it is being invaded. The doorbell starts ringing at noon the next day. I ignore it. They're going to come in anyway, and I might as well not do any more than I have to. I sit in boxer shorts with my feet up on my desk, a cup of coffee in front of me, and Rage Against the Machine cranked as loud as my stereo can manage. My bedroom is going to be an uncomfortable place to visit.

From over my shoulder I hear a voice yell. "Can we see this room!?!?"

I glance backward to see an Asian couple and what must be two or three of their friends following the real estate agent. I wave them in and immediately switch songs. As they cross my room to the bathroom, Blue Oyster Cult erupts from the speakers.

Oh no, there goes Tokyo!
Go, go Godzilla!

The agent snaps her head at me and I take another swig of coffee. This pattern continues through the afternoon, the doorbell ringing and me causing whatever havoc I can. One couple is cautioned not to open the pantry door because I don't want the rat to get out before I can set a trap. Why can't I turn down the music? Because I am making an old school mix tape, that's why. Later in the day a middle-aged woman is escorted inside. "Is that the hooker?' I ask. "You know I don't like them that old. Take her to the back though, and I'll get to her in a minute."

Another agent makes an appointment for two o'clock the next afternoon. I claw through my closet for an old Halloween costume. At 1:55 PM, I hide in full ninja regalia, sword in hand, behind the entertainment center in the living room. The doorbell rings twice, and, when no one answers, the agent lets herself and her clients in.

"Aaaaarrrgh!" I scream, leaping out of my corner and into the middle of the room, my katana flashing through the air in a circle. I land with the blade held threateningly in front of me, and then I stand there silently, staring them down.

The clients, an older couple, clutch at their chests. Their agent is breathing heavily next to them. I pause for another moment and then sheathe my sword and pull my mask off. "I totally thought you were someone else," I say, and casually walk back to my room and lock the door.

A half hour later my phone rings. "What the hell do you think you're doing?" Janet yells through the phone.

"Exactly what I said I would do."

"You don't have the right—"

"I do have the right. Until it sells I maintain all the rights that my lease provides me, including the right to the 'quiet enjoyment' of my property, and just so you're aware Janet, I'm quite enjoying this."

"Can we talk about this?"

"Nope. We could have talked about this yesterday, but some-one didn't want to have a conversation. Remember? So I am going to spend my day the way I want to, and that way doesn't include a bathroom full of Japanese people."

The viewings dwindle after that. I replace the lock on my bed-room door with one that is impenetrable, and I am prepared to set booby traps if the lock doesn't hold. I have already reached the conclusion that I have no moral issues with crushing an agent or a prospective buyer with a large rolling boulder. Invading my pri-vacy might have to end with a poison dart to the neck.

With my room secured, my roommate and I begin looking for a new place to live. House shopping is an exhaustive process; online pictures don't truly represent the place you visit, and you have to look at 103 properties before you even find one that fits in the "maybe" category. Then, after a month of not finding anything worthy of committing to, my roommate informs me that he is going to move back in with his father.

"I don't want to hose you on this, but it's sort of an offer I can't say no to," he tells me. "I want to be out of here as quickly as I can." I am caught completely off guard.

The next morning I make an appointment to go see what looks like a tiny apartment in the pictures. What I said about the pictures not being representative earlier? I'm not exaggerating. The place is just a kitchen. The agent has taken pictures of the four different walls and labeled them as different rooms.

There is room for a full-size bed, as long as you have no plans to open the refrigerator door. There is one closet, which is nice, as it means there will be somewhere to put a small television. Even hanging artwork on the walls will mean cutting into the square footage. It is awful. And the entire apartment is on a slant. People really live like this?

The agent and I walk back outside so we will have room to shake hands. "This really isn't going to work," I tell him. "But thanks."

"I figured as much. Look, I wouldn't normally bring this up, but I do know something that might be a little more your speed," he says. A mortgage broker in his office happens to have a garage apartment that isn't being leased out. It isn't even on the market, and it is big: a living room, dining room, full bath, kitchen, washer and dryer, a garage for my car and space for my motorcycle. "And he'd rent it out for the same price as the shithole I just showed you," the agent says.

The place is better than described and in a great neighborhood. I will make up in gas money anything I am losing by not having a roommate. I will have privacy too, which is priceless. I am thrilled to not have to defend myself from strangers twice a day with aggressive music and ninja costumes.

Not that I ever mind dressing like a ninja. I suppose that is the only good part about having home invaders. Then again, when you have a place to yourself, you can dress like a ninja anytime you want.

I DIDN'T KILL YOUR FRIEND

I despise rituals of any sort, but despite my best efforts I still cling to a few. Coffee for instance. Even in the most foreign country or on the longest camping trip, my body will not creak and grind its way to life without at least one cup. After two hours of sleep or twenty, I have to drag my useless carcass to a carafe before I can even breathe properly.

It's my last week in this house, and I am lazily enjoying a cup of Kona and the final few days of morning solitude instead of packing. I have a picture window over the sink that looks out into my backyard, and usually that yard is full of birds. Every day at first light, blue jays, mockingbirds, cardinals, and yellow-throated warblers all compete for real estate in the branches of the white oak while the rest huddle around the perimeter and wait for an open spot. It is the Wal-Mart parking lot of the avian world.

My grandmother used to throw loaves of bread to the birds in her backyard when I was growing up. I would stand and watch them land en masse, and that interest has somehow followed me into adulthood. The birds have always reminded me of miniature, carnivorous dinosaurs prancing around and feasting on brontosauruses made of dough. It almost makes me jealous. They look like dinosaurs, their food is there waiting when they show up, *and* they get to fly? It is serene and honest to me, and I observe them still with the wonder of a seven-year old.

This morning though, it is quiet. The gold-green glow of the sunlight on the foliage makes its way through the window as I watch the coffee pot drip its way closer to full. Nothing moves outside. The silence is perfect and peaceful. There is no thriller-movie crescendo of music to warn me that anything is about to occur. All is simply silent.

And then I hear it hit.

SMACK!

I don't even get a chance to see what it is before it disappears, but it sounds like someone has thrown a baseball at the house. I shoot outside to find the saddest little brown-and-yellow bird I've ever seen. After bouncing off the glass, he has landed sloppily on top of the bush below. My first instinct is that he is just disoriented, but then he looks up at me, coughs a little dramatic cough, and then flops his head to the side, dead.

Cough, cough. Flop.

It is a bit overacted honestly, and kind of fake looking. It is the way I would expect William Shatner to die. He has apparently broken his neck on impact, and he just lays there, limp and crooked. I pick him up to make sure that he isn't just pretending, and then I walk his body out to the middle of the yard. I am not exactly sure what to do with a dead bird. As I set him down, I can hear fluttering in the branches above. I am being watched. Judged. "I didn't kill your friend," I say. "Weren't you watching?"

And then I start to wonder what caused this in the first place. The obvious explanation is that the bird simply didn't know there was a window in his way and flew into it accidentally. I mean, birds do seem pretty dumb. I wouldn't necessarily put this below a bird. Unwilling to let Occam's razor explain this away though, my mind wanders. What had really taken place here?

Did the other birds dare this young chick to do it? Maybe he was trying to get into some feathered fraternity — Better Than Ezra's *Desperately Wanting* performed live in the animal kingdom.

Maybe there was an emergency and he was recklessly trying to get home to solve the crisis. Maybe one of his eggs had fallen down the stairs or his wife had broken her hollow little hip and he was racing to provide aid.

Or was he drinking? I know I've done a lot of dumb things after a few drinks. Maybe he ate some fermented fruit. It is entirely possible that he was just fucked up and all the other birds warned him not to fly, and as usual he didn't listen. "No, no, no. I'm fine. I'm just going up the block. I only live like two trees away. I'll call you when I get there."

Or was he a daredevil bird that pushed things too far? I can relate. I tore my ACL when I was 18 jumping over a table to win a $10 bet. I'm painfully aware that bad things happen. Maybe this bird, flirting with death, got caught up in the moment and took things past the limit. "I'll go out doing what I love," he told himself, then tucked his wings in tightly and closed his eyes.

What if this particular bird was a twin and his brother had kept him locked away in an iron mask for years. Now, angry and frustrated, he was on a mission to get revenge. Suddenly, catching a glimpse of his reflection and seeing what he could only assume was his evil doppelgänger brother, he attacked. Wait, that's not how that movie happened at all.

Or had war been declared and I am simply unaware? Perhaps it was a kamikaze strategy employed by the Bird Nation — my kitchen window becoming a clear-paned USS Bunker Hill to the bird's Ensign Ogawa. On that note, maybe it was a more traditional suicide. Perhaps he was picked on in bird school and just couldn't take it anymore. Maybe he knew the easiest way for a bird to kill himself would be to hit a window at 30 mph. Now, somewhere off amongst the limbs, a press conference was being held. "He wasn't that kind of kid," his mother would cry.

They'll say he was desensitized by the abundance of violence in bird cinema, or that he used to play that video game where you steal another bird's wings and run from the blue jays; that somehow he just didn't grasp the concept that a window will really kill you. Bird society will be blamed for making death seem so simple and small. Thank God he just killed himself, others will say. He could have taken out an entire nest if he'd wanted to.

All of the possibilities aside, I'm having a hard time letting go of the idea that he was just a really stupid bird that couldn't tell a reflection from the real world; that the echoing impact that rattled its way through my kitchen was just Darwin being Darwin. "No breeding for you, you simple-minded little sack of down. Here's a window. Eat it. You heard the man! Life's got to move on, chick-adee, and you're in the way. Somebody sweep up these feathers. Move along. There's nothing to see here."

There is no note. Whatever it was that drove that little bird to hurl his own body against the side of my house, only he will ever know for sure.

And he's not saying a word.

DOGS OF WAR

Character is supposedly what we display in times of crisis or when no one's watching or some other strange, dumb set of criteria. Once again I have been plagued by visitors in the night, sent to attack me and me alone. Determined, I believe, to see how I respond. And not simply the nightstalking mosquito either, this is a well-orchestrated, surgical attack. It feels like a psychology experiment gone bad, like the Milgram Experiment or that Stanford Prison thing. Maybe not that bad, but I still feel as if I'm being toyed with.

I lie in bed at night and I hear them coming. Whispers and clicks in the dark, the invaders peer through the inky black and wait for exhaustion to drag me into an uneasy sleep. They organize and plot and look for the perfect opening, and then they come for my socks.

These fucking squirrels.

The pillaging squirrels — and a rooster — are the only drawbacks to where I live now. My new place is comfortable. All of my stuff fits exactly as it should fit. My bookshelf is full of the volumes I've collected in the last year, punctuated by 1,000 trinkets and memories from my travels. My desk sits on one side of the living room, my dual monitors surrounded by speakers. It is a place where I can get stuff done. My bedroom faces north so the sunlight is constant. I opted not to put up blackout curtains so that it would jar me out of bed and into productivity on most mornings. My brilliant plan to surface at eight or nine has been preempted though.

My apartment sits isolated from my neighbors in the middle of four intersecting backyards and one of those backyards is home to the rooster. A rooster, a rooster, a motherfucking rooster, inside the loop in Houston, Texas.

It's more elusive than one would expect a rooster to be, too. It is borderline ninja, and I know this because I've tried to kill it. I've never been hunting and I'm a total sucker for animals of any sort. I could cause harm to a human much more easily than I ever could an animal, but then again this is not a human standing in the backyard cockadoodledoo-ing seven days a week at 5:00 AM.

The woman that owns that house is bat-shit crazy. She won't answer her door for me, or for the police. For all I know, she could be dead herself. The wooden fence around her yard is painted with bright red hearts and catchy little hippie phrases like, "Animals Are People Too!" and, "One Planet, One Love." The sign on the door that I have beaten on every morning for the last month reads, "I maintain this house for the comfort of my cats. If you can't deal with that, you can't deal with me."

She places the welfare of these animals above my own and for that I hate this woman. She is a hopeless PETA-head, and that is why I bought the slingshot. I've collected a good number of small rocks (ball bearings would look too much like evidence) and from my bathroom window I can see into her backyard. The rooster prances up and down a particular path, hidden almost entirely behind the branches of a low-hanging tree. He is confident behind his barricade, but that hasn't stopped me from rifling pebble after pebble through the leaves in an attempt to hit him. Of course he knows this and waits for me to shut the window and give up, then he runs up to the fence and lets out another mad cackle before darting back to the cover of the brush. THWOP, THWOP, THWOP. Three more rocks rip through the air and hit nothing. "Goddamn bird!" I yell. "I'm gonna shoot you in your little rooster face."

I want to drag its carcass to the hippie's doorstep and bang away until she's forced to answer. "Looks like people can be animals, too!" I'll say, with wild eyes and chicken blood running down my arms. What criminal mind houses a yard full of birds and a house full of cats with such disregard for others? Probably the kind of person that would raise an army of attack squirrels. I bet my invaders are the product of her animal friendly lifestyle as well. She probably hand-fed them and took them in, and now that she has 63 cats, they need a new place to hang out. Hence the velvet rope and the bouncer outside the squirrel dance club that my attic has become.

And now I am not safe inside.

A few days ago I woke up to the morning crowing and stumbled into the kitchen to make coffee. Bleary-eyed and headachy, I poured my first cup. As I started to gain my focus I noticed a sock hanging out from under the counter. And not a full pair either. Just one. "Did something happen last night that I don't remember?" I think to myself. "Why would I take my socks off in the kitchen? Did I try to put them in the cabinet? Did I come home with Paul McCartney's wife? This makes no sense."

Pulling the sock out from the opening underneath the base board, I noticed that it has several holes in it. "Squirrels," I growl. I've known they were here for a while. It's an older place, and there are plenty of openings that allow them into the attic. I hear them constantly but I've remained unconcerned. Once I knew that they weren't mice or rats — the piles of nuts in the attic and the sight of actual squirrels hopping from the power lines onto my roof cinched that — I just resigned myself to being the provider of winter refuge for the fuzzy little things.

But now they're taunting me. They're literally stealing my socks, as if my clothes dryer wasn't already doing enough of that. They are decisive. To get my socks requires some investigation. While I will occasionally leave a pair lying in the living room (one of the perks of bachelorhood), they usually end up in my bedroom. None of my other clothes are touched, nor are the dish towels or the beanie I left lying on my desk or the bag of Cheetos Puffs on top of my microwave. They're selective little creatures. It takes determination to say no to those Cheetos. Cheetos are delicious.

They seem content to only drag the socks as far as the holes under the cabinets too. They don't take them all the way inside, but leave them hanging out just enough to let me know they were here. It's a form of counting coup, I'm afraid. And this is why I feel I'm being experimented on. It's as if they know that I am incapable of simply trapping them or killing them. They want to see how I'll react. They know that boredom will entice me to fight back. I have moved anything cloth-like to my bedroom now and I make sure the door is shut when I leave. Then I place one sock strategically in the middle of my dining room floor before I make my exit or turn in for the night. I have to know if they come, and come they do, but never when I can see them.

I sit on my couch and stare like a child waiting for Santa. My eyes finally close involuntarily, but only briefly, snapping open again to find the sock tucked neatly in its cubbyhole under the sink. "How the hell did you do that?!" I yell. Somewhere a squirrel rolls around on the floor laughing and high-fiving his friends. I rip the sock out from the hole and throw it back on the floor. "I'm going to bed, you bastard!" I yell at nothing whatsoever. "Come get your stupid sock if you want it!" Then I wake up the next morning to find it sitting exactly where I left it. It's no fun for them if I don't care.

So I have to formulate a plan before I go out of town again. I have to get rid of them. I don't know if I am up against one rogue animal or 100. In my mind, my walls and my attic are now one big Squirrel Kingdom. Buttons and thimbles and scores of socks line the halls of a *Secret of NIMH* world. Will taking one of these creatures out be enough? Should I trap one and leave it bound in the middle of my kitchen floor as a warning to other squirrels? Should I poison a sock? Buy an owl? I don't know what to do.

I do know that the gauntlet has been thrown down. They started this thing with the socks. "Cry Havoc," I say, "and let slip the dogs of war!" Maybe that's the answer. Actual dogs. Or a fox. A fox would eat the squirrels *and* the rooster. I want to put on face paint and get a ghillie suit and hide with my slingshot. I want to set up a box and a stick with a string tied to one of my socks. I want a jet pack and some rocket skates and I want to paint a fake tunnel on my wall like Wile E. Coyote. I want to put the squirrels and the rooster and all their little friends in one big bag and toss it into the ocean — and then blow up the ocean.

I want to win.

Maybe I should focus on the flower child in the house behind me, maybe point my slingshot at her instead. Cut off the head and the monster dies, right? Who takes their animals that seriously? Seriously. These things are interrupting my lifestyle, and her desire to protect them only makes me angrier. She is a rodent-whispering mastermind, a Squirrel Queen who clicks and whistles at her horde until they cross the fence line and do her bidding.

I want to cook steak with my windows open so she has to smell it. And I want a fur coat. And I want to beat a baby seal over the head with a penguin in her driveway. Her "Save the Animals" mission has clearly had the opposite effect on me.

But for now, I will continue to type, stopping every sentence or two to pause my music and glance into the kitchen and try to catch a glimpse of the cocky little rodent as it mocks me. Because right now I am clearly not winning. Right now I am losing.

And badly.

I can hear the squirrels flitting back and forth on the roof. I can hear the rooster too, cluck-cluck-clucking just feet outside of my apartment. I cut my eyes across the desk to the slingshot. "I could go outside and kill them all right now," I think, bloodthirsty.

And I would, too, if only I could find a pair of socks.

EPILOGUE:
WE ARE NOT
THE MACHINE

I am fascinated by the way the internet has impacted our culture. It used to anger me until I realized that I am a product of the very same living, breathing connectivity that I profess to despise. The web has proven a great equalizer, particularly in the area of art, which isn't always what I feel the world needs. The cream doesn't always rise to the top in this oversaturated digital realm where any kid with a cheap guitar can record a rock album. You can't sift through the new releases in any medium, like you could even ten or fifteen years ago.

What I do relish is that the web has given some truly talented people a way to reach an audience that didn't exist before. They no longer have to wait for a publisher or a record label or a network to sign off on them — which is great because those corporate people don't know shit to begin with — but can instead throw themselves into the sea of consumers all on their own, sink or swim.

Not just the exceptional is allowed through however. With no one checking IDs at the door, anyone can explode overnight. I'm staggered when the Rebecca Blacks and the Gangnam Styles or even the Justin Biebers break through the surface and become household names. Kardashians. Kids making a million bucks a year for playing video games or putting together Legos. I get baffled and incredulous. It honestly makes me want to quit what I am doing. If that is what the people want, then I sincerely missed my exit.

But it's a digital world, man. The cross section that thinks those *American Idol* kids can actually sing is not as big as it used to be. We're smarter than that. We have infinite information, access to technology, and permission to plug directly into the brains of seven billion people in a piece of a fraction of a sliver of a second. No longer are we resigned to muttering to ourselves on the couch that we could do a better job.

All those dorky boys and girls from high school that couldn't compete with the cool kids? Well, they went out and leveled the playing field, and now we all get to play on it. Who cares if a major studio won't buy your script? For a few thousand dollars you can shoot it yourself. You can write a book and have a hard copy of it in your hands within the week. The big men in their suits and ties, with their meetings and their rules and their dumb little criteria, they're obsolete.

It is total chaos on the internet and it's incredible. What started as a series of posts on my website — rants read only by me and maybe three girls in my little Texas town — quickly moved to MySpace. A year later, out of thousands and thousands of blogs, virtually everything I wrote began to land in the Top 20. I had an audience. I pushed my site from the stage as I toured around the country. I started a mailing list. I began to take it seriously, and in return it started to take me seriously.

Then MySpace collapsed in upon itself, losing out to the Facebook giant. In search of a new home, I began writing for the Los Angeles-based online magazine *The Nervous Breakdown*, and, surrounded by people far more talented than myself, I was forced to again reevaluate how seriously I took my writing. Somehow, through all of that, the stories in this book were born.

But it's the internet that did it. That's the part I can't get around. It feels like a deal with the Devil, really. This ocean of digital jetsam is the sole reason I ever managed to peck out an entire book. The communities in that swirling mass pushed me to write, and then pushed me to get better, and then pushed me again to complete a bigger project. There is good at the center of that storm, I've found.

I've been introduced to wonderful writers over this electronic landscape. Comedians, authors, filmmakers, and wordsmiths all frequent these online taverns where we commune. We trade ideas and send drunken emails back and forth, and comment and critique as we search for validation amongst our peers. And it works.

Whatever that process is, we police ourselves and build completely intangible cities where we can ply our trades. We have opened doors to rooms that we couldn't have imagined a decade or two ago. All of the physical boundaries are gone. We are limited by absolutely nothing. The positives almost make all those cookie-cutter success stories digestible.

B ut we still have a long way to go. The most unsavory aspect of the web is that people still get to be anonymous. Not being held accountable for what you say is apparently quite liberating. Chat rooms, message boards, social networking — all of it brings out sides of people that you would never see in person. Aggression, hate, racism, and fanaticism all bubble up to the surface from behind the safety of the computer screen.

It all finds its way onto the internet. White people use racial slurs like commas, with complete disregard for history because there are no repercussions online, while other races spew machine gun-like hate from their own corners.

There should be a reality show that tracks these IP addresses, kidnaps the people behind the screen names, and locks them together in a Thunderdome. Along with those fucking squirrels. That might be the only way you could get me to watch Reality TV actually.

The information comes at us faster than we could ever hope to process it. It used to be the Top 10 of the week; now what's hot changes by the hour. And we digest all of it, incapable of separating the true from the manufactured, and once it's bounced through our filters, we regurgitate it back into the same frothing pool we snatched it from.

Just picture things that get copied and pasted and forwarded without any substantiation whatsoever. We've become little bouncing rubber balls of conformity that jump on whatever ship left the harbor with the most passengers that day, and it's sort of funny. Actually, it's really funny.

We have this amazing tool of connectivity that allows for the free exchange of ideas, and instead of using it to solve problems or enlighten, we use it to post unsubstantiated political bullshit and links to pictures of cats that can't spell. Not that there's anything wrong with mindless entertainment — I got blindsided by Candy Crush years ago, and I stay logged into Instagram, and Reddit remains my productivity's arch nemesis — but that seems to be all we're doing with it.

I like getting sucked into intelligent debate between people. Not the screaming match, flame wars, but true dialogue and conversations full of fresh ideas and new ways of looking at problems.

I'm fully aware that I don't know a lot of things about a lot of things. Still, I have my opinions and I do enjoy having them challenged. It's the only way to make sure they hold up, and the only way to intelligently change one's mind on occasion.

So have at it, I say. Not just on the web, but with all of it. We won, whether we know it or not. No longer are we subjected to only the whims of the rich men in charge. We can watch, read, listen to, and create anything we want.

We are not the machine. We are something totally different and very much alive. We can legitimately, finally, communicate with each other without their permission. We have more power to change the world than any president or pope ever will. If there is going to be a revolution in how we function as a people, it won't start at the top; it will start on the front line.

And this, my friends, is the front line.

ACKNOWLEDGMENTS

First, to my mom, who never once cared that I was venturing down unproven paths. As unorthodox as my life has been, you only cared that what I did made me happy. I don't know if every kid understands how much of a blessing that is, but in trusting me to be myself, you gave me one of the greatest gifts a parent can give a child. And yes, you can have credit for at least part of my sense of humor. Or blame. It's a fuzzy line.

To The Whiskey Brothers, Rob Mungle and Sam Demaris. Sam, you have been there for more of my nonsense than any human being should be subjected to. I don't know if you killed a child in another life, but if I am your karmic reward, it must have been bad. Let's never get stuck in Yemen again.

Paul Harris, who dragged me to the beach and made me write what would become the first finished chapter. To Jes, for all of it. You pushed me to start this more times than you should have, but exactly as many times as I needed.

Sarah Bell for editing my nightmare. Thank you for recognizing how close to it I was, and for making me clarify and delete and hate myself in the process. There's a lot of you in here.

Brad Listi and that wonderful group of misfits at The Nervous Breakdown. My dearest Erika Rae and Megan DiLullo. Also Richard Cox, Uche Ogbuji, and Duke Haney (for making the comments a competitive thing, which eventually made me write both better and more often).

To Jamie Blaine. Through your comments and personal messages, you did more to bolster my confidence inside that circle of brilliant writers than you could ever possibly know. You single-handedly might be more responsible for this than anyone.

To those of you who find yourself mentioned in these pages. Some of you made it in with your identities intact, and in other cases, names have been changed to protect the guilty.

And finally, to all of you who read this in one incarnation or another over the years. You are far too numerous to name, but each of you, in different, tiny ways, are responsible for this ever seeing print. You know exactly who you are.

ABOUT THE AUTHOR

Slade Ham is a comedian, writer, explorer, and pilot of Houston's infamous *The Whiskey Brothers*. He has performed in 47 countries on 6 continents. One day he hopes to host a travel show as he continues to trick the world into paying him to do the things he loves. When he's not killing dragons and drinking whiskey, he maintains a very expensive storage unit in Houston, TX.